THE UK NINJA DUAL ZONE AIR FRYER COOKBOOK

1800 Days of Nutritious & Healthy Recipes to Fry, Roast and Bake Meals for the Whole family using UK Measurements and Ingredients

Jesse Hartmann

Legal & Disclaimer

The content and information in this book is consistent and truthful, and it has been provided for informational, educational and business purposes only.

The illustrations in the book are from the website shutterstock.com, depositphoto.com and freepik.com and have been authorized.

The content and information contained in this book has been compiled from reliable sources, which are accurate based on the knowledge, belief, expertise and information of the Author. The author cannot be held liable for any omissions and/or errors.

TABLE OF CONTENT

INTRODUCTION

Welcome to the world of dual-zone cooking with the Ninja Foodi Dual Zone Air Fryer! This cookbook is your gateway to exploring the incredible capabilities of this innovative kitchen appliance.

With its advanced technology and unique design, the Ninja Foodi Dual Zone Air Fryer allows you to cook two different dishes simultaneously, without any cross-flavour contamination. It's like having two separate cooking appliances in one, giving you the freedom to create complete meals with ease and efficiency.

In this cookbook, you'll discover a wide range of tantalizing recipes designed specifically for the Ninja Foodi Dual Zone Air Fryer. From crispy appetizers and succulent mains to delightful desserts and everything in between, each recipe is crafted to showcase the versatility and culinary excellence this appliance has to offer.

Whether you're a seasoned home cook or just starting your culinary journey, this cookbook will inspire you to push the boundaries of your cooking skills. With step-by-step instructions, helpful tips, and creative flavour combinations, you'll be able to create impressive dishes that will delight your taste buds and impress your family and friends.

So, get ready to unlock the full potential of your Ninja Foodi Dual Zone Air Fryer and embark on a flavourful adventure that will take your cooking to new heights. Let's dive in and start creating delicious memories in the kitchen!

CHAPTER 1

GETTING STARTED TO NINJA FOODI DUAL ZONE AIR FRYER

The Ninja Foodi Dual Zone Air Fryer is a versatile kitchen appliance that combines the benefits of air frying with the convenience of two independent cooking zones. With its sleek design and user-friendly features, it offers a simple and efficient way to prepare delicious meals for your family and friends.

Featuring six cooking functions including air fry, max crisp, roast, bake, reheat, and dehydrate, this appliance allows you to explore a variety of culinary possibilities. Whether you want to enjoy crispy fries, succulent roasts, or healthy dehydrated snacks, the Ninja Foodi Dual Zone Air Fryer has got you covered.

The dual zone cooking feature enables you to cook two different dishes simultaneously, with individual temperature and time settings for each zone. This means you can prepare a complete meal with different cooking requirements, saving you time and effort in the kitchen.

In addition to its cooking versatility, the Ninja Foodi Dual Zone Air Fryer is designed with easy cleaning in mind. The non-stick, dishwasher-safe drawers and crisper plates make cleanup a breeze, so you can spend less time on maintenance and more time enjoying your delicious creations.

Whether you're a seasoned chef or just starting out in the kitchen, the Ninja Foodi Dual Zone Air Fryer offers a convenient and efficient way to cook your favorite meals. With its compact size and user-friendly controls, it seamlessly fits into your kitchen and simplifies your cooking process.

Experience the joy of healthier, flavourful meals with the Ninja Foodi Dual Zone Air Fryer - a kitchen companion that brings ease, versatility, and deliciousness to your everyday cooking.

Benefits of Ninja Foodi Dual Zone Air Fryer

Discover the benefits of the Ninja Foodi Dual Zone Air Fryer and elevate your cooking experience to new heights. From healthier meals to time-saving convenience, this appliance offers a multitude of advantages:

- **Versatile Cooking**

The Ninja Foodi Dual Zone Air Fryer offers a wide range of cooking functions, allowing you to air fry, max crisp, roast, bake, reheat, and dehydrate. It's like having multiple appliances in one, providing endless culinary possibilities.

- **Dual Zone Capability**

With two independent cooking zones, you can simultaneously cook different dishes with individual temperature and time settings. This saves time and enables you to create complete meals without compromising on taste or texture.

- **Energy Efficiency**

Compared to conventional ovens, the Ninja Foodi Dual Zone Air Fryer can help you save up to 75% on your energy bill when using the air fry function. It's a more energy-efficient way to cook without sacrificing flavour or quality.

- **Healthier Cooking**

The air frying function of the Ninja Foodi Dual Zone Air Fryer allows you to enjoy crispy and delicious food with up to 75% less fat compared to deep frying. It's a healthier alternative that still delivers satisfying results.

- **Spacious Capacity**

With its generous cooking capacity, the appliance can easily accommodate 4-6 portions. Whether you're cooking for a small family or hosting a dinner party, the Ninja Foodi Dual Zone Air Fryer has you covered.

- **Easy Cleanup**

The non-stick, dishwasher-safe drawers and crisper plates make cleaning up a breeze. You can spend less time scrubbing and more time enjoying your meal.

- **Precise Control**

The intuitive control panel with temperature and time adjustments allows you to have full control over your cooking. Achieve the perfect level of crispiness, tenderness, and flavour every time.

- **Space-Saving Design**

The compact size of the Ninja Foodi Dual Zone Air Fryer ensures that it won't take up too much countertop space. It's designed to fit seamlessly into your kitchen, making it a convenient addition to your cooking routine.

Cooking Functions and Control Panel

The Ninja Foodi Dual Zone Air Fryer offers a range of cooking functions and a user-friendly control panel, allowing you to effortlessly create a variety of delicious meals.

Cooking Functions

Here are the cooking functions and their corresponding features:

Max Crisp: The Max Crisp function is perfect for achieving that extra crispy texture on your favorite foods. Whether it's French fries, chicken nuggets, or onion rings, this function ensures a satisfying crunch with minimal oil.

Air Fry: The Air Fry function is your go-to option for healthier frying. It circulates hot air around the food, creating a crispy exterior while retaining moisture inside. You can achieve deliciously golden results with significantly less oil compared to traditional frying methods.

Roast: Utilize the Roast function to cook tender meats, poultry, and vegetables to perfection. This function mimics the effects of a conventional oven, giving you succulent results with a crispy outer layer.

Bake: With the Bake function, you can indulge in a wide variety of baked treats and desserts. From fluffy cakes to mouthwatering pastries, this function ensures even heat distribution for consistent and delicious results.

Reheat: The Reheat function allows you to revive leftovers and enjoy them as if they were freshly cooked. By gently warming your food, it brings back the desired texture and crispiness, providing a quick and convenient meal.

Dehydrate: Harness the Dehydrate function to create healthy and flavourful snacks. This function removes moisture from fruits, vegetables, and meats, preserving their nutrients while intensifying their natural flavours.

Control Panel

The control panel of the Ninja Foodi Dual Zone Air Fryer is designed to simplify your cooking experience. Here are the key features of the control panel:

Power Button: Turn the appliance on or off with a single press of the power button.

Zone Buttons: Select the desired cooking zone (Zone 1 or Zone 2) to adjust settings independently for each drawer.

Temperature Arrows: Use the up and down arrows to adjust the cooking temperature according to your recipe requirements.

Time Arrows: Adjust the cooking time by using the up and down arrows, allowing you to customise the duration for each cooking session.

Sync Button: Automatically synchronize the cook times of both zones, ensuring that your dishes finish cooking simultaneously.

Match Button: Match the settings of Zone 2 to those of Zone 1 for cooking larger quantities of the same food or different foods requiring the same settings.

Start/Stop Button: Initiate the cooking process by pressing the Start button, and stop or pause the cooking cycle as needed.

The intuitive control panel and clear function buttons make it effortless to navigate and customise your cooking settings with precision. Experiment with different functions and unleash your culinary creativity with the Ninja Foodi Dual Zone Air Fryer.

How to Use the Appliance and Its Key Features

Using the Ninja Foodi Dual Zone Air Fryer is a breeze, and its key features enhance your cooking experience. Here's a step-by-step guide to help you make the most of this incredible appliance:

1. Preparing the Appliance

Before you start cooking, ensure that the appliance is clean and dry. Make sure the drawers and crisper plates are in place and securely inserted. It's important to read the user manual for specific instructions on setup and safety guidelines.

2. Selecting Cooking Functions

The Ninja Foodi Dual Zone Air Fryer offers six cooking functions: air fry, max crisp, roast, bake, reheat, and dehydrate. Choose the appropriate function for your desired dish. Each function has its own unique settings to achieve optimal results.

3. Adjusting Temperature and Time

Use the temperature arrows to set the desired cooking temperature. The time arrows allow you to adjust the cooking time according to your recipe's requirements. The control panel gives you precise control over the cooking process, ensuring perfect results every time.

4. Dual Zone Cooking

Take advantage of the dual zone feature by using both drawers simultaneously. Each drawer has its own temperature and time settings, allowing you to cook two different dishes at once. This is ideal for preparing complete meals or catering to different tastes.

5. Sync and Match Functions

The Sync button ensures that both zones finish cooking at the same time, even if they have different cook times. The Match button allows you to replicate the settings of one zone to the other, simplifying the process when cooking larger quantities or similar foods.

6. Start the Cooking Process

Once you have set the desired temperature and time, press the start/stop button to begin cooking. The appliance will start heating up, and the countdown timer will begin.

7. Monitoring the Cooking Progress

Throughout the cooking process, keep an eye on your food. Check the progress to ensure it is cooking evenly and adjust the temperature or time if needed. The Ninja Foodi Dual Zone Air Fryer gives you the flexibility to make adjustments during cooking.

8. Cleaning and Maintenance

After you have finished cooking and the appliance has cooled down, clean the drawers and crisper plates. These components are dishwasher safe for easy cleanup. Remember to follow the manufacturer's instructions for cleaning and maintenance to keep your appliance in optimal condition.

By following these simple steps and utilizing the key features of the Ninja Foodi Dual Zone Air Fryer, you can effortlessly create delicious meals for yourself and your loved ones. Explore the versatility and convenience that this appliance offers, and unleash your culinary creativity with confidence.

Cleaning & Maintenance

To ensure the longevity and optimal performance of your Ninja Foodi Dual Zone Air Fryer, regular cleaning and maintenance are vital. Follow these simple steps to keep your appliance in top shape:

Unplug the Appliance: Before cleaning, always unplug the appliance from the power source. This ensures your safety and prevents any accidental mishaps.

Allow the Appliance to Cool: Give the appliance ample time to cool down before cleaning. This prevents the risk of burns and allows for safe handling.

Clean the Exterior: Use a soft, damp cloth to wipe the exterior surfaces of the appliance. Pay attention to any stubborn stains or food residue. Avoid using abrasive cleaners or harsh chemicals that may damage the finish.

Wash the Drawers and Accessories: The drawers and accessories of the Ninja Foodi Dual Zone Air Fryer are dishwasher safe. Alternatively, you can wash them by hand with warm, soapy water. Ensure thorough cleaning to remove any grease, food particles, or stains.

Soak for Stubborn Residue: If there are stubborn residues on the drawers or accessories, soaking them in warm, soapy water can help loosen the grime. Allow them to soak for a short period, then gently scrub with a non-abrasive sponge or brush.

Rinse and Dry Thoroughly: After cleaning, rinse the drawers and accessories with clean water to remove any soap residue. Ensure they are completely dry before reassembling or storing to prevent the growth of mold or mildew.

Wipe the Control Panel: Use a soft, slightly damp cloth to wipe the control panel. Avoid getting excessive moisture into the control panel area to prevent damage to the electronic components.

Regular Maintenance Checks: Periodically inspect the appliance for any signs of wear, damage, or loose parts. If you notice any issues, contact the manufacturer or authorized service center for assistance or to arrange for repairs.

Store Properly: When not in use, store the Ninja Foodi Dual Zone Air Fryer in a clean, dry place. Ensure that the appliance is protected from dust and moisture.

By following these cleaning and maintenance practices, you can keep your Ninja Foodi Dual Zone Air Fryer in optimal condition, ensuring it continues to deliver delicious meals for you and your loved ones. Remember to consult the user manual for specific care instructions provided by the manufacturer.

Troubleshooting Common Issues

While the Ninja Foodi Dual Zone Air Fryer is designed to provide hassle-free cooking, you may encounter some common issues along the way. Here are some troubleshooting tips to help you overcome them:

1. **Appliance Not Powering On**

- Ensure the appliance is properly plugged into a functioning power outlet.
- Check if the power cord is securely connected to the appliance.
- Confirm that the outlet is working by plugging in another device.
- If the issue persists, contact the manufacturer for further assistance.

2. **Uneven Cooking**

- Make sure you are distributing the food evenly in the drawers, avoiding overcrowding.
- Consider using the Match function to ensure both zones cook at the same temperature and time.
- Rotate or flip the food halfway through the cooking process for more consistent results.

3. **Food Not Crispy**

- Adjust the cooking time and temperature based on the desired crispness.
- Consider using the Max Crisp function for extra crispiness.
- Ensure that the food is adequately dried before air frying to avoid excess moisture.

4. **Excessive Smoke**

- Check if there is any food debris or grease buildup in the appliance. Clean it thoroughly.
- Avoid using excessive oil or greasy ingredients, as they can cause smoke.
- Ensure that the appliance is placed in a well-ventilated area during operation.

5. **Error Messages on Display**

- If you encounter an error message, consult the user manual for specific troubleshooting steps.
- In case the issue persists, contact the manufacturer's customer service for further assistance.

6. **Unusual Noises**

- Some operational noises are normal, but if you notice any unusual or loud sounds, check for loose parts or foreign objects in the appliance.
- Contact the manufacturer or authorized service center if the noise continues or seems abnormal.

7. **Overheating**

- Make sure the appliance is not placed near flammable materials or other heat-sensitive objects.
- Check that the vents are not blocked, as this can cause overheating.
- Allow the appliance to cool down if it becomes too hot before using it again.

If you encounter any other issues or if the troubleshooting steps provided do not resolve the problem, it is recommended to contact the manufacturer's customer service for further guidance. They will be able to assist you with specific troubleshooting tailored to your appliance.

Conclusion

The Ninja Foodi Dual Zone Air Fryer is a versatile and efficient appliance that brings convenience and deliciousness to your kitchen. With its innovative design and multiple cooking functions, it offers a range of culinary possibilities for you to explore.

Throughout this cookbook, we have highlighted the numerous benefits of using the Ninja Foodi Dual Zone Air Fryer. From its ability to cook two different foods simultaneously to its energy-saving capabilities, this appliance is truly a game-changer in your cooking routine.

With the Ninja Foodi Dual Zone Air Fryer, you can unleash your culinary creativity, prepare mouthwatering meals, and impress your family and friends with your cooking prowess. So, get ready to embark on a culinary adventure filled with flavourful dishes, crispy delights, and healthy options, all made possible by the power of the Ninja Foodi Dual Zone Air Fryer.

Happy cooking and enjoy the delectable delights that await you with the Ninja Foodi Dual Zone Air Fryer!

CHAPTER 2
BREAKFAST

Delish Mushroom Frittata

SERVES: 2

PREP TIME: 15 minutes
COOK TIME: 17 minutes

½ red onion, sliced thinly
300 g button mushrooms, sliced thinly
3 eggs
Cooking spray, as required
45 g feta cheese, crumbled
15 ml olive oil
Salt, to taste

1. Grease two 10 cm ramekins with cooking spray.
2. Heat olive oil on medium heat in a frying pan and add onion and mushrooms.
3. Sauté for about 5 minutes and dish out the mushroom mixture in a bowl.
4. Whisk together eggs and salt in a small bowl and transfer into the prepared ramekins.
5. Place the mushroom mixture over the eggs and top with feta cheese.
6. Insert a crisper plate in both drawers. Place one ramekin in each drawer.
7. Select Zone 1, select BAKE, set temperature to 160°C, and set time to 12 minutes. Select MATCH COOK to match Zone 2 settings to Zone 1. Select START/PAUSE to begin cooking.
8. When cooking is complete, transfer ramekins and serve warm.

Parmesan Ranch Risotto

SERVES: 2

PREP TIME: 10 minutes
COOK TIME: 30 minutes

15 ml olive oil
1 clove garlic, minced
15 g unsalted butter
1 onion, diced
175 g Arborio rice
480 ml chicken stock, boiling
50 g Parmesan cheese, grated

1. Grease a 18 x 13 cm baking dish with olive oil and stir in the garlic, butter, and onion.
2. Install a crisper plate in Zone 1 drawer. Place baking dish in the drawer, then insert drawer in unit.
3. Select Zone 1, select BAKE, set temperature to 200°C, and set time to 30 minutes. Press the START/PAUSE button to begin cooking.
4. With 26 minutes remaining, press START/PAUSE to pause the unit. Remove the drawer from unit and add the rice. Reinsert drawer in unit and press START/PAUSE to resume cooking.
5. With 22 minutes remaining, press START/PAUSE to pause the unit. Remove the drawer from unit and pour in the chicken stock. Reinsert drawer in unit, turn the air fryer to 160°C and press START/PAUSE to resume cooking.
6. When cooking is complete, scatter with cheese and serve.

Fast Coffee Doughnuts

SERVES: 6

PREP TIME: 5 minutes
COOK TIME: 8 minutes

50 g sugar
½ tsp. salt
120 g flour
5 g baking powder
60 ml coffee
1 tbsp. aquafaba
15 ml sunflower oil

1. In a large bowl, combine the sugar, salt, flour, and baking powder.
2. Add the coffee, aquafaba, and sunflower oil and mix until a dough is formed. Leave the dough to rest in and the refrigerator.
3. Remove the dough from the fridge and divide up, kneading each section into a doughnut.
4. Insert a crisper plate in both drawers. Place half of the doughnuts in a single layer in each drawer.
5. Select Zone 1, select BAKE, set temperature to 200°C, and set time to 8 minutes. Select MATCH COOK to match Zone 2 settings to Zone 1. Select START/PAUSE to begin cooking.
6. When cooking is complete, transfer doughnuts to a plate. Serve warm.

Tasty Toasts

SERVES: 4

PREP TIME: 10 minutes
COOK TIME: 6 minutes

4 bread slices
225 g ricotta cheese
115 g smoked salmon
1 shallot, sliced
40 g rocket
1 garlic clove, minced
1 tsp. lemon zest
¼ tsp. freshly ground black pepper

1. Insert a crisper plate in both drawers. Place 2 bread slices in a single layer in each drawer.
2. Select Zone 1, select BAKE, set temperature to 180°C, and set time to 6 minutes. Select MATCH COOK to match Zone 2 settings to Zone 1. Select START/PAUSE to begin cooking.
3. When cooking is complete, transfer bread slices to a plate.
4. Put garlic, ricotta cheese and lemon zest in a food processor and pulse until smooth.
5. Spread this mixture over each bread slice and top with salmon, rocket and shallot.
6. Sprinkle with black pepper and serve warm.

Spinach with Scrambled Eggs

SERVES: 2

PREP TIME: 10 minutes
COOK TIME: 10 minutes

30 ml olive oil
4 eggs, whisked
140 g fresh spinach, chopped
1 medium tomato, chopped
5 ml fresh lemon juice
½ tsp. coarse salt
½ tsp. ground black pepper
16 g fresh basil, roughly chopped

1. Grease a 18 x 13-cm baking pan with the oil, tilting it to spread the oil around.
2. Add the remaining ingredients, apart from the basil leaves, whisking well until everything is completely combined.
3. Install a crisper plate in Zone 1 drawer. Place baking pan in the drawer, then insert drawer in unit.
4. Select Zone 1, select BAKE, set temperature to 175°C, and set time to 10 minutes. Press the START/PAUSE button to begin cooking.
5. When cooking is complete, top with fresh basil leaves before serving.

Jacket Potatoes

SERVES: 2

PREP TIME: 5 minutes
COOK TIME: 30 minutes

2 potatoes
15 g mozzarella cheese, shredded
15 g butter, softened
1 tsp. chives, minced
3 g fresh parsley, chopped
45 g sour cream
Salt and black pepper, to taste

1. Prick the potatoes with a fork.
2. Install a crisper plate in Zone 1 drawer. Place potatoes in the drawer, then insert drawer in unit.
3. Select Zone 1, select AIR FRY, set temperature to 200°C, and set time to 30 minutes. Press the START/PAUSE button to begin cooking.
4. With 15 minutes remaining, press START/PAUSE to pause the unit. Remove the drawer from unit and flip the potatoes over. Reinsert drawer in unit and press START/PAUSE to resume cooking.
5. When cooking is complete, remove drawer from unit. Transfer potatoes to a plate.
6. Mix together remaining ingredients in a bowl until well combined.
7. Cut the potatoes from the centre and stuff in the cheese mixture.
8. Serve immediately.

Apple and Walnut Muffins

MAKES 8 MUFFINS

PREP TIME: 15 minutes
COOK TIME: 10 minutes

120 g flour
70 g sugar
5 g baking powder
1 g baking soda
¼ tsp. salt
2 g cinnamon
¼ tsp. ginger
¼ tsp. nutmeg
1 egg
40 g pancake syrup
40 g melted butter
180 g unsweetened apple sauce
½ tsp. vanilla extract
30 g chopped walnuts
30 g diced apple

1. In a large bowl, stir together the flour, sugar, baking powder, baking soda, salt, cinnamon, ginger, and nutmeg.
2. In a small bowl, beat egg until frothy. Add syrup, butter, apple sauce, and vanilla and mix well.
3. Pour egg mixture into dry ingredients and stir just until moistened.
4. Gently stir in nuts and diced apple.
5. Divide batter among 8 parchment-paper-lined muffin cups.
6. Insert a crisper plate in both drawers. Place 4 muffin cups in each drawer.
7. Select Zone 1, select BAKE, set temperature to 165°C, and set time to 10 minutes. Select MATCH COOK to match Zone 2 settings to Zone 1. Select START/PAUSE to begin cooking, until toothpick inserted in centre comes out clean.
8. Serve warm.

Luscious Scrambled Eggs

SERVES: 2

PREP TIME: 10 minutes
COOK TIME: 10 minutes

30 g unsalted butter
4 eggs
30 g fresh mushrooms, chopped finely
30 g Parmesan cheese, shredded
30 g tomato, chopped finely
Salt and black pepper, to taste

1. Grease a 18 x 13-cm baking pan.
2. Whisk together eggs with salt and black pepper in a bowl.
3. Melt butter in the baking pan and add whisked eggs, mushrooms, tomatoes and cheese.
4. Install a crisper plate in Zone 1 drawer. Place the baking pan in the drawer, then insert drawer in unit.
5. Select Zone 1, select BAKE, set temperature to 150°C, and set time to 10 minutes. Press the START/PAUSE button to begin cooking.
6. When cooking is complete, remove drawer from unit. Serve warm.

Bacon Eggs on the Go

SERVES: 1

PREP TIME: 5 minutes
COOK TIME: 15 minutes

2 eggs
115 g bacon, cooked
Salt and ground black pepper, to taste

1. Put liners in a regular cupcake tin.
2. Crack an egg into each of the cups and add the bacon. Season with some pepper and salt.
3. Install a crisper plate in Zone 1 drawer. Place 2 cups in the drawer, then insert drawer in unit.
4. Select Zone 1, select AIR FRY, set temperature to 200°C, and set time to 15 minutes. Press the START/PAUSE button to begin cooking, until the eggs are set.
5. When cooking is complete, remove drawer from unit. Serve warm.

Breakfast Creamy Doughnuts

SERVES: 8

PREP TIME: 10 minutes
COOK TIME: 16 minutes

cooking spray
60 g butter, softened and divided
2 large egg yolks
350 g plain flour
7 g baking powder
1 pinch baking soda
75 g caster sugar
2 g cinnamon
100 g sugar
1 tsp. salt
120 g sour cream

1. Mix together sugar and butter in a bowl and beat until crumbly mixture is formed.
2. Whisk in the egg yolks and beat until well combined.
3. Sift together flour, baking powder, baking soda and salt in another bowl.
4. Add the flour mixture and sour cream to the sugar mixture.
5. Mix well to form a dough and refrigerate it.
6. Roll the dough into 5 cm thickness and cut the dough in half.
7. Coat both sides of the dough with the melted butter.
8. Insert a crisper plate in both drawers. Spray with cooking spray. Place one dough in each drawer.
9. Select Zone 1, select Bake, set temperature to 180°C, and set time to 16 minutes. Select MATCH COOK to match Zone 2 settings to Zone 1. Select START/PAUSE to begin cooking.
10. When cooking is complete, sprinkle the doughnuts with the cinnamon and caster sugar to serve.

Maple Oat Coconut Flax Granola

SERVES: 4

PREP TIME: 15 minutes
COOK TIME: 30 to 45 minutes

2 tbsps. avocado oil
2 tbsps. unsweetened finely desiccated coconut
2 tbsps. ground almonds
2 tbsps. flax seed
2 tbsps. maple syrup
¼ tsp. vanilla extract
2 tbsps. brown rice flour
Pinch sea salt
75 g rolled oats

1. Combine the oil, coconut, ground almonds, flax seed, and maple syrup in a food processor, process until smooth.
2. Pour the mixture into a bowl and stir in the vanilla, flour, and salt. Stir in the oats.
3. Evenly spread the mixture in the inner pot and press Bake and cook at 180°C for 30 to 45 minutes, turning every 15 minutes, until golden brown. After baking, allow to cool. Store in an airtight container.

Herbed Breakfast Bean Sausage

SERVES: 4

PREP TIME: 20 minutes
COOK TIME: 30 minutes

1 small onion, quartered
2 garlic cloves
1 carrot, peeled and cut into large chunks
½ tsp. fennel seeds
Water, as needed
400 g tinned pinto beans, drained
1 tbsp. nutritional yeast
1 tbsp. almond flour
½ tsp. dried oregano (1 tsp. fresh)
1 tsp. smoked paprika
½ tsp. dried thyme (1 tsp. fresh)
½ tsp. dried sage (1 tsp. fresh)
½ tsp. dried basil (1 tsp. fresh)
½ tsp. sea salt

1. Use a silicone mat or greaseproof paper to line the inner pot.
2. Add the onion, garlic, and carrot in a food processor. Chop until fine, or use hand to chop.
3. Add the onion-carrot mixture, and the fennel seeds into the Ninja Foodi, press Sear/Sauté and cook at 200°C for about 4 minutes or until the vegetables are soft, adding water if needed. Remove from the heat and allow to cool.
4. Add the pinto beans to the food processor, pulse until roughly chopped, but not to a paste. Add the onion-carrot mixture to the processor, and process until blended.
5. Pour the contents into a medium bowl. Add the yeast, almond flour, oregano, paprika, thyme, sage, basil, and salt. Mix until combined.
6. Measure 4 tbsps. of sausage and use your hand to shape into a patty. Then place each patty into the inner pot carefully. Continue with the remaining sausage.
7. Press Bake and cook at 205°C for 25 to 30 minutes, until crispy on the outside but still moist on the inside.
8. After baking, remove from the basket and allow to cool for a few minutes and serve.

Vegan Baked Portobello with Avocado

SERVES: 2

PREP TIME: 10 minutes
COOK TIME: 20 minutes

2 tbsps. olive oil
¼ tsp. salt
½ tsp. cayenne pepper
1 tsp. dried oregano
2 tsps. dried basil
2 Portobello mushroom caps
½ of avocado, sliced
75 g purslane

1. Prepare the marinade, in a small bowl, add the oil, salt, cayenne pepper, oregano, and basil and stir until mixed.
2. Use a foil to line a baking sheet, brush with oil, arrange with the mushroom caps, evenly pour the marinade over the mushroom caps and allow them to marinate for 10 minutes.
3. Press Bake and cook the mushroom caps at 220°C for 20 minutes, flipping halfway, until tender and cooked.
4. After baking, transfer the mushroom caps onto two plates, top with the avocado and purslane evenly and serve.

Banana Breakfast Bars

SERVES: 2

PREP TIME: 10 minutes
COOK TIME: 10 minutes

1 banana
1 tbsp. agave nectar
65 g spelt flour
1/16 tsp. sea salt
50 g quinoa flakes
Extra:
60 ml grapeseed oil
120 ml blackberry jam

1. In a medium bowl, add the peeled burro bananas and use a fork to mash them.
2. Add the oil and agave nectar to the bowl, stir until well combined, and then stir in the flour, salt, and quinoa flakes until a sticky dough comes together.
3. Use parchment paper to line Crisp Plate, spread two-third of the prepared dough in its bottom, layer with blackberry jam, and place the remaining dough on the top.
4. Press Bake and cook at 180°C for 10 minutes and then allow the dough to cool for 15 minutes.
5. Cut the dough into four bars and serve.

Easy Baked Chickpea Falafel

SERVES: 6

PREP TIME: 15 minutes, plus overnight
COOK TIME: 30 minutes

200 g dried chickpeas
20 g chopped fresh coriander (or parsley if preferred)
½ chopped brown onion
20 g chopped fresh parsley
3 garlic cloves, peeled
1½ tbsps. chickpea flour or wheat flour (if gluten is not a concern)
1 tsp. ground coriander
½ tsp. baking powder
2 tsps. ground cumin
2 tbsps. freshly squeezed lemon juice

1. The night before making falafel, add the dried chickpeas in a large bowl, pour in the water to cover by 7 cm. Cover the bowl and allow to soak for at least 8 hours or overnight. Drain.
2. Use greaseproof paper to line the inner pot.
3. Combine the soaked chickpeas and the remaining ingredients in a high-speed blender or food processor. Pulse until all ingredients are well combined but not smooth, it should have the consistency of sand but stick together when pressed.
4. Divide the falafel mixture into 20 balls with a cookie dough scoop or two spoons and place them in the inner pot. Lightly flatten each ball using the bottom of a measuring cup. This will help them cook more evenly.
5. Press Bake and cook at 190°C for 15 minutes. Flip and bake for another 10 to 15 minutes, until lightly browned.
6. Place in an airtight container and refrigerate for up to 1 week or freeze for up to 1 month.

Classic British Breakfast

SERVES: 2

PREP TIME: 5 minutes
COOK TIME: 20 minutes

240 g potatoes, sliced and diced
400 g baked beans
2 eggs
15 ml olive oil
1 sausage
Salt, to taste

1. Break the eggs onto a 18 x 13-cm baking dish and sprinkle with salt.
2. Lay the beans on the dish, next to the eggs.
3. In a bowl, coat the potatoes with the olive oil. Sprinkle with salt.
4. Insert a crisper plate in both drawers. Place potato slices in the Zone 1 drawer, then insert drawer in unit. Place the dish in the Zone 2 drawer, then insert drawer in unit.
5. Select Zone 1, select AIR FRY, set temperature to 200°C, and set time to 20 minutes. Select Zone 2, select BAKE, set temperature to 190°C, and set time to 16 minutes. Select SYNC. Press the START/PAUSE button to begin cooking.
6. When the Zone 1 and 2 times reach 5 minutes, press START/PAUSE to pause the unit. Remove the drawers from unit. Slice up the sausage and throw the slices on top of the beans and eggs. Reinsert drawers in unit and press START/PAUSE to resume cooking.
7. When cooking is complete, serve immediately.

Easy Sausage Pizza

SERVES: 4

PREP TIME: 10 minutes
COOK TIME: 6 minutes

30 ml ketchup
1 pitta bread
80 g sausage
225 g Mozzarella cheese
1 tsp. garlic powder
15 ml olive oil

1. Spread the ketchup over the pitta bread.
2. Top with the sausage and cheese. Sprinkle with the garlic powder and olive oil.
3. Install a crisper plate in Zone 1 drawer. Place pizza in the drawer, then insert drawer in unit.
4. Select Zone 1, select BAKE, set temperature to 170°C, and set time to 6 minutes. Press the START/PAUSE button to begin cooking.
5. When cooking is complete, remove drawer from unit. Serve warm.

CHAPTER 3
POULTRY

Chicken with Broccoli ······ 20
Oats Crusted Chicken Breasts ······ 20
Air-Fried Chicken Wings ······ 21
Appetising Chicken ······ 21
Sweet and Spicy Chicken Drumsticks ······ 22
Buffalo Chicken Wings ······ 22
Air Fried Crispy Chicken Tenders ······ 23
Honey Glazed Chicken Drumsticks ······ 23
Chicken with Apple ······ 24
Pecan-Crusted Turkey Cutlets ······ 24
Mini Turkey Meatloaves with Carrot ······ 25
Cajun Chicken Thighs ······ 25
Sausage Stuffed Chicken ······ 26

Chicken with Broccoli

SERVES: 3

PREP TIME: 20 minutes
COOK TIME: 20 minutes

450 g boneless, skinless chicken breasts, sliced
180 g small broccoli florets
20 g butter
1½ tbsps. dried parsley, crushed
½ tbsp. onion powder
½ tbsp. garlic powder
¼ tsp. red chilli powder
¼ tsp. paprika

1. Mix the butter, parsley and spices in a bowl.
2. Coat the chicken slices and broccoli generously with the spice mixture.
3. Insert a crisper plate in both drawers. Place marinated chicken slices in the Zone 1 drawer, then insert drawer in unit. Place broccoli in the Zone 2 drawer, then insert drawer in unit.
4. Select Zone 1, select AIR FRY, set temperature to 190°C, and set time to 20 minutes. Select Zone 2, select AIR FRY, set temperature to 200°C, and set time to 15 minutes. Select SYNC. Press the START/PAUSE button to begin cooking.
5. When the Zone 1 and 2 times reach 8 minutes, press START/PAUSE to pause the unit. Remove the drawers from unit and shake for 10 seconds. Reinsert drawers in unit and press START/PAUSE to resume cooking.
6. When cooking is complete, serve chicken with broccoli.

Oats Crusted Chicken Breasts

SERVES: 2

PREP TIME: 20 minutes
COOK TIME: 22 minutes

2 (170 g) chicken breasts
75 g oats
3 g fresh parsley
2 medium eggs
Salt and black pepper, to taste
28 g mustard powder

1. Season the chicken pieces with salt and black pepper and keep aside.
2. Put the oats, mustard powder, parsley, salt and black pepper in a blender and pulse until coarse.
3. Place the oat mixture into a shallow bowl and whisk the eggs in another bowl.
4. Dredge the chicken in the oat mixture and dip into the whisked eggs.
5. Install a crisper plate in Zone 1 drawer. Place chicken breasts in the drawer, then insert drawer in unit.
6. Select Zone 1, select AIR FRY, set temperature to 190°C, and set time to 22 minutes. Press the START/PAUSE button to begin cooking.
7. With 10 minutes remaining, press START/PAUSE to pause the unit. Remove the drawer from unit and flip the chicken breasts over. Reinsert drawer in unit and press START/PAUSE to resume cooking.
8. When cooking is complete, remove drawer from unit. Transfer chicken breasts to a plate. Serve warm.

Air-Fried Chicken Wings

SERVES: 6

PREP TIME: 5 minutes
COOK TIME: 30 minutes

900 g chicken wings, tips removed
⅛ tsp. salt

1. Season the wings with salt.
2. Install a crisper plate in Zone 1 drawer. Place the wings in the drawer, then insert drawer in unit.
3. Select Zone 1, select AIR FRY, set temperature to 200°C, and set time to 30 minutes. Press the START/PAUSE button to begin cooking.
4. With 15 minutes remaining, press START/PAUSE to pause the unit. Remove the drawer from unit and flip the wings over. Reinsert drawer in unit and press START/PAUSE to resume cooking.
5. When cooking is complete, remove drawer from unit. Transfer the wings to a plate. Serve warm.

Appetising Chicken

SERVES: 2

PREP TIME: 30 minutes
COOK TIME: 18 minutes

340 g chicken pieces
3 g fresh rosemary, chopped
1 lemon, cut into wedges
1 tsp. ginger, minced
15 ml soy sauce
7 ml olive oil
15 ml oyster sauce
45 g coconut sugar

1. Mix chicken, ginger, soy sauce and olive oil in a bowl.
2. Marinate and refrigerate for about 30 minutes.
3. Install a crisper plate in Zone 1 drawer. Place chicken in the drawer, then insert drawer in unit.
4. Select Zone 1, select AIR FRY, set temperature to 200°C, and set time to 18 minutes. Press the START/PAUSE button to begin cooking.
5. Meanwhile, mix the remaining ingredients in a small bowl.
6. With 10 minutes remaining, press START/PAUSE to pause the unit. Remove the drawer from unit. Spread the sauce over the chicken. Squeeze juice from lemon wedges over chicken and top with the wedges. Reinsert drawer in unit and press START/PAUSE to resume cooking.
7. When cooking is complete, remove drawer from unit. Transfer chicken to a plate. Serve warm.

Sweet and Spicy Chicken Drumsticks

SERVES: 4

PREP TIME: 15 minutes
COOK TIME: 22 minutes

4 (170 g) chicken drumsticks
1 garlic clove, crushed
15 ml mustard
8 g brown sugar
1 tsp. cayenne pepper
1 tsp. red chilli powder
Salt and ground black pepper, as required
15 ml vegetable oil

1. Mix garlic, mustard, brown sugar, oil, and spices in a bowl.
2. Rub the chicken drumsticks with marinade and refrigerate for about 30 minutes.
3. Install a crisper plate in Zone 1 drawer. Place drumsticks in the drawer, then insert drawer in unit.
4. Select Zone 1, select AIR FRY, set temperature to 200°C, and set time to 22 minutes. Press the START/PAUSE button to begin cooking.
5. With 10 minutes remaining, press START/PAUSE to pause the unit. Remove the drawer from unit and flip the drumsticks over. Reinsert drawer in unit and press START/PAUSE to resume cooking.
6. When cooking is complete, remove drawer from unit. Transfer drumsticks to a plate. Serve warm.

Buffalo Chicken Wings

SERVES: 6

PREP TIME: 20 minutes
COOK TIME: 30 minutes

900 g chicken wings, cut into drumettes and flats
1 tsp. chicken seasoning
1 tsp. garlic powder
Ground black pepper, to taste
15 ml olive oil
60 ml red hot sauce
30 ml low-sodium soy sauce

1. Season each chicken wing evenly with chicken seasoning, garlic powder, and black pepper.
2. Install a crisper plate in Zone 1 drawer. Place chicken wings in the drawer and drizzle with olive oil, then insert drawer in unit.
3. Select Zone 1, select ROAST, set temperature to 200°C, and set time to 30 minutes. Press the START/PAUSE button to begin cooking.
4. With 15 minutes remaining, press START/PAUSE to pause the unit. Remove the drawer from unit. Pour the red hot sauce and soy sauce on the chicken wings and toss to coat well. Reinsert drawer in unit and press START/PAUSE to resume cooking.
5. When cooking is complete, remove drawer from unit. Transfer chicken wings to a plate. Serve warm.

Air Fried Crispy Chicken Tenders

SERVES: 3

PREP TIME: 20 minutes
COOK TIME: 24 minutes

2 (170 g) boneless, skinless chicken breasts, pounded into 1-cm thickness and cut into tenders
60 g plain flour
180 g panko breadcrumbs
30 g Parmesan cheese, finely grated
2 large eggs
7 ml Worcestershire sauce, divided
180 ml buttermilk
½ tsp. smoked paprika, divided
Salt and ground black pepper, as required

1. Mix buttermilk, ¾ tsp. of Worcestershire sauce, ¼ tsp. of paprika, salt, and black pepper in a bowl.
2. Combine the flour, remaining paprika, salt, and black pepper in another bowl.
3. Whisk the egg and remaining Worcestershire sauce in a third bowl.
4. Mix the panko breadcrumbs and Parmesan cheese in a fourth bowl.
5. Put the chicken tenders into the buttermilk mixture and refrigerate overnight.
6. Remove the chicken tenders from the buttermilk mixture and dredge into the flour mixture.
7. Dip into the egg and coat with the breadcrumb mixture.
8. Insert a crisper plate in both drawers. Place half of the chicken tenders in a single layer in each drawer.
9. Select Zone 1, select AIR FRY, set temperature to 200°C, and set time to 24 minutes. Select MATCH COOK to match Zone 2 settings to Zone 1. Select START/PAUSE to begin cooking.
10. When the Zone 1 and 2 times reach 12 minutes, press START/PAUSE to pause the unit. Remove the drawers from unit and flip the chicken tenders over. Reinsert drawers in unit and press START/PAUSE to resume cooking.
11. When cooking is complete, transfer chicken tenders to a plate. Serve warm.

Honey Glazed Chicken Drumsticks

SERVES: 4

PREP TIME: 15 minutes
COOK TIME: 25 minutes

½ tbsp. fresh rosemary, minced
3 g fresh thyme, minced
4 (170 g) boneless chicken drumsticks
60 ml Dijon mustard
15 ml honey
30 ml olive oil
Salt and black pepper, to taste

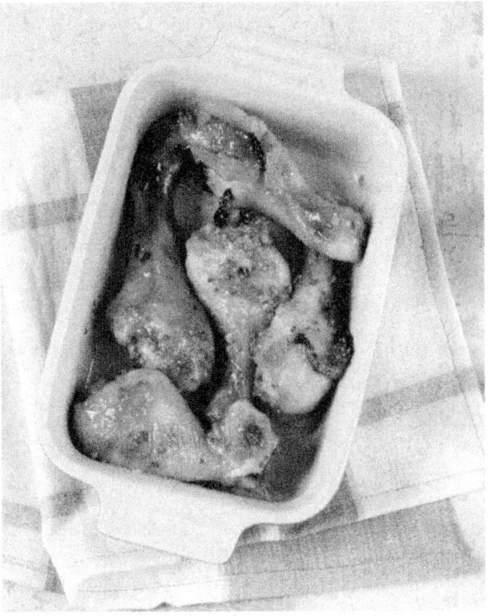

1. Mix mustard, honey, oil, herbs, salt, and black pepper in a bowl.
2. Rub the chicken drumsticks with marinade and refrigerate overnight.
3. Install a crisper plate in Zone 1 drawer. Place drumsticks in the drawer, then insert drawer in unit.
4. Select Zone 1, select ROAST, set temperature to 160°C, and set time to 25 minutes. Press the START/PAUSE button to begin cooking.
5. With 10 minutes remaining, press START/PAUSE to pause the unit. Remove the drawer from unit and flip the drumsticks over. Reinsert drawer in unit. Set the Air fryer to 180ºC and press START/PAUSE to resume cooking.
6. When cooking is complete, remove drawer from unit. Transfer drumsticks to a plate. Serve warm.

Chicken with Apple

SERVES: 8

PREP TIME: 10 minutes
COOK TIME: 20 minutes

1 shallot, thinly sliced
1 tsp. fresh thyme, minced
2 (115 g) boneless, skinless chicken thighs, sliced into chunks
1 large apple, cored and cubed
6 g fresh ginger, finely grated
120 ml apple cider
30 ml maple syrup
Salt and black pepper, as required

1. Mix the shallot, ginger, thyme, apple cider, maple syrup, salt, and black pepper in a bowl.
2. Coat the chicken generously with the marinade and refrigerate to marinate for about 8 hours.
3. Insert a crisper plate in both drawers. Place chicken pieces in the Zone 1 drawer, then insert drawer in unit. Place cubed apples in the Zone 2 drawer, then insert drawer in unit.
4. Select Zone 1, select AIR FRY, set temperature to 200°C, and set time to 20 minutes. Select Zone 2, select AIR FRY, set temperature to 200°C, and set time to 15 minutes. Select SYNC. Press the START/PAUSE button to begin cooking.
5. When the Zone 1 and Zone 2 times reach 10 minutes, press START/PAUSE and remove drawers from unit. In Zone 1, flip the chicken pieces over. In Zone 2, shake for 10 seconds. Reinsert drawers in unit and press START/PAUSE to resume cooking.
6. When cooking is complete, serve chicken with apples.

Pecan-Crusted Turkey Cutlets

SERVES: 4

PREP TIME: 10 minutes
COOK TIME: 15 minutes

75 g panko bread crumbs
¼ tsp. salt
¼ tsp. pepper
¼ tsp. dry mustard
¼ tsp. poultry seasoning
50 g pecans
30 g cornflour
1 egg, beaten
450 g turkey cutlets, 1-cm thick
Salt and pepper, to taste
Cooking spray

1. Place the panko crumbs, salt, pepper, mustard, and poultry seasoning in a food processor. Process until crumbs are finely crushed. Add pecans and process just until nuts are finely chopped.
2. Place cornflour in a shallow dish and beaten egg in another. Transfer coating mixture from food processor into a third shallow dish.
3. Sprinkle turkey cutlets with salt and pepper to taste.
4. Dip cutlets in cornflour and shake off excess, then dip in beaten egg and finally roll in crumbs, pressing to coat well. Spray both sides with cooking spray.
5. Insert a crisper plate in both drawers. Place 2 cutlets in a single layer in each drawer.
6. Select Zone 1, select AIR FRY, set temperature to 190°C, and set time to 15 minutes. Select MATCH COOK to match Zone 2 settings to Zone 1. Select START/PAUSE to begin cooking.
7. When the Zone 1 and 2 times reach 8 minutes, press START/PAUSE to pause the unit. Remove the drawers from unit and flip the cutlets over. Reinsert drawers in unit and press START/PAUSE to resume cooking.
8. When cooking is complete, transfer cutlets to a plate. Serve warm.

Mini Turkey Meatloaves with Carrot

SERVES: 4

PREP TIME: 6 minutes
COOK TIME: 22 minutes

50 g minced onion
30 g grated carrot
2 garlic cloves, minced
20 g ground almonds
10 ml olive oil
1 tsp. dried marjoram
1 egg white
340 g turkey breast, minced

1. In a medium bowl, stir together the onion, carrot, garlic, almonds, olive oil, marjoram, and egg white.
2. Add the minced turkey. With your hands, gently but thoroughly mix until combined.
3. Double 16 foil muffin cup liners to make 8 cups. Divide the turkey mixture evenly among the liners.
4. Insert a crisper plate in both drawers. Place 4 cups in a single layer in each drawer.
5. Select Zone 1, select AIR FRY, set temperature to 200°C, and set time to 22 minutes. Select MATCH COOK to match Zone 2 settings to Zone 1. Select START/PAUSE to begin cooking.
6. When cooking is complete, transfer the turkey meatloaves to a plate. Serve warm.

Cajun Chicken Thighs

SERVES: 4

PREP TIME: 15 minutes
COOK TIME: 25 minutes

60 g plain flour
1 egg
4 (115 g) skin-on chicken thighs
1½ tbsps. Cajun seasoning
1 tsp. seasoning salt
450 g green beans, trimmed and halved
5 g unsalted butter, melted
¼ tsp. garlic powder

1. Mix the flour, Cajun seasoning and salt in a bowl.
2. Whisk the egg in another bowl and coat the chicken thighs with the flour mixture.
3. Dip into the egg and dredge again into the flour mixture.
4. Mix the green beans, butter and garlic powder in a medium bowl and toss to coat well.
5. Insert a crisper plate in both drawers. Place chicken thighs in the Zone 1 drawer, skin side down, then insert drawer in unit. Place green beans in the Zone 2 drawer, then insert drawer in unit.
6. Select Zone 1, select AIR FRY, set temperature to 200°C, and set time to 25 minutes. Select Zone 2, select AIR FRY, set temperature to 200°C, and set time to 15 minutes. Select SYNC. Press the START/PAUSE button to begin cooking.
7. When the Zone 1 and 2 times reach 8 minutes, press START/PAUSE to pause the unit. Remove the drawers from unit and shake for 10 seconds. Reinsert drawers in unit and press START/PAUSE to resume cooking.
8. When cooking is complete, serve chicken thighs with green beans.

Sausage Stuffed Chicken

SERVES: 4

PREP TIME: 10 minutes
COOK TIME: 22 minutes

4 (115 g) skinless, boneless chicken breasts
4 sausages, casing removed
30 ml mustard sauce

1. Roll each chicken breast with a rolling pin for about 1 minute.
2. Arrange 1 sausage over each chicken breast and roll up. Secure with toothpicks.
3. Install a crisper plate in Zone 1 drawer. Place stuffed chicken breasts in the drawer, then insert drawer in unit.
4. Select Zone 1, select AIR FRY, set temperature to 190°C, and set time to 22 minutes. Press the START/PAUSE button to begin cooking.
5. With 10 minutes remaining, press START/PAUSE to pause the unit. Remove the drawer from unit and flip the chicken breasts over. Reinsert drawer in unit and press START/PAUSE to resume cooking.
6. When cooking is complete, remove drawer from unit. Transfer chicken breasts to a plate and serve with mustard sauce.

CHAPTER 4

FISH AND SEAFOOD

Garlic-Lemon Tilapia······28
Mahi Mahi with Green Beans······28
Homemade Fish Fingers······29
Glazed Halibut Steak······29
Spicy Orange Prawns······30
Crispy Cod Cakes with Salad Greens······30
Juicy Salmon and Asparagus······31
Amazing Salmon Fillets······31
Sesame Seeds Coated Tuna with Spinach······32
Ranch Tilapia······32
Southern Style Catfish······33
Crispy Cod Sticks······33
Cod with Prawns and Pasta······34

Garlic-Lemon Tilapia

SERVES: 4

PREP TIME: 5 minutes
COOK TIME: 15 minutes

15 ml lemon juice
15 ml olive oil
1 tsp. minced garlic
½ tsp. chilli powder
4 (170 g) tilapia fillets

1. In a large, shallow bowl, mix together the lemon juice, olive oil, garlic, and chilli powder to make a marinade. Place the tilapia fillets in the bowl and coat evenly.
2. Insert a crisper plate in both drawers. Place 2 tilapia fillets in a single layer in each drawer, leaving space between each fillet.
3. Select Zone 1, select AIR FRY, set temperature to 200°C, and set time to 15 minutes. Select MATCH COOK to match Zone 2 settings to Zone 1. Select START/PAUSE to begin cooking, until the fish is cooked and flakes easily with a fork.
4. When cooking is complete, transfer tilapia fillets to a plate. Serve warm.

Mahi Mahi with Green Beans

SERVES: 4

PREP TIME: 15 minutes
COOK TIME: 15 minutes

500 g green beans
2 tbsps. fresh dill, chopped
4 (170 g) Mahi Mahi fillets
15 ml avocado oil
Salt, as required
2 garlic cloves, minced
30 ml fresh lemon juice
15 ml olive oil

1. Combine garlic, dill, lemon juice, salt and olive oil in a bowl. Coat Mahi Mahi in this garlic mixture.
2. Mix the green beans, avocado oil and salt in a large bowl.
3. Insert a crisper plate in both drawers. Place Mahi Mahi in the Zone 1 drawer, then insert drawer in unit. Place green beans in the Zone 2 drawer, then insert drawer in unit.
4. Select Zone 1, select AIR FRY, set temperature to 200°C, and set time to 15 minutes. Select MATCH COOK to match Zone 2 settings to Zone 1. Press the START/PAUSE button to begin cooking.
5. When cooking is complete, serve Mahi Mahi immediately with green beans.

Homemade Fish Fingers

SERVES: 4

PREP TIME: 15 minutes
COOK TIME: 15 minutes

4 fish fillets
60 g whole-wheat flour
1 tsp. seasoned salt
2 eggs
120 g whole-wheat panko bread crumbs
½ tbsp. dried parsley flakes
Cooking spray

1. Cut the fish fillets lengthwise into "sticks."
2. In a shallow bowl, mix the whole-wheat flour and seasoned salt.
3. In a small bowl, whisk the eggs with 1 tsp. of water.
4. In another shallow bowl, mix the panko bread crumbs and parsley flakes.
5. Coat each fish stick in the seasoned flour, then in the egg mixture, and dredge them in the panko bread crumbs.
6. Insert a crisper plate in both drawers. Place half of fish fingers in a single layer in each drawer.
7. Select Zone 1, select AIR FRY, set temperature to 200°C, and set time to 15 minutes. Select MATCH COOK to match Zone 2 settings to Zone 1. Select START/PAUSE to begin cooking.
8. When the Zone 1 and 2 times reach 8 minutes, press START/PAUSE to pause the unit. Remove the drawers from unit and flip the fish sticks over. Lightly spray with the cooking spray. Reinsert drawers in unit and press START/PAUSE to resume cooking.
9. When cooking is complete, transfer fish fingers to a plate. Serve warm.

Glazed Halibut Steak

SERVES: 4

PREP TIME: 30 minutes
COOK TIME: 15 minutes

cooking spray
450 g haddock steak
1 garlic clove, minced
¼ tsp. fresh ginger, grated finely
120 ml low-sodium soy sauce
60 ml fresh orange juice
30 ml lime juice
120 ml cooking wine
40 g sugar
¼ tsp. red pepper flakes, crushed

1. Put all the ingredients except haddock steak in a pan and bring to a boil.
2. Cook for about 4 minutes, stirring continuously and remove from the heat.
3. Put the haddock steak and half of the marinade in a resealable bag and shake well.
4. Refrigerate for about 1 hour and reserve the remaining marinade.
5. Insert a crisper plate in both drawer and spray with cooking spray. Place half of the haddock steaks in a single layer in each drawer.
6. Select Zone 1, select AIR FRY, set temperature to 200°C, and set time to 15 minutes. Select MATCH COOK to match Zone 2 settings to Zone 1. Select START/PAUSE to begin cooking.
7. When the Zone 1 and 2 times reach 7 minutes, press START/PAUSE to pause the unit. Remove the drawers from unit and flip the haddock steaks over. Reinsert drawers in unit and press START/PAUSE to resume cooking.
8. When cooking is complete, transfer haddock steaks to a plate. Coat with the remaining glaze and serve hot.

Spicy Orange Prawns

SERVES: 4

PREP TIME: 20 minutes
COOK TIME: 10 minutes

80 ml orange juice
3 tsps. minced garlic
1 tsp. Old Bay seasoning
¼ to ½ tsp. cayenne pepper
450 g medium prawns, peeled and deveined, with tails off
Cooking spray

1. In a medium bowl, combine the orange juice, garlic, Old Bay seasoning, and cayenne pepper.
2. Dry the prawns with paper towels to remove excess water.
3. Add the prawns to the marinade and stir to evenly coat. Cover with clingfilm and place in the refrigerator for 30 minutes so the prawn can soak up the marinade.
4. Install a crisper plate in Zone 1 drawer and spray lightly with cooking spray. Place prawns in the drawer, then insert drawer in unit.
5. Select Zone 1, select AIR FRY, set temperature to 200°C, and set time to 10 minutes. Press the START/PAUSE button to begin cooking.
6. With 5 minutes remaining, press START/PAUSE to pause the unit. Remove the drawer from unit. Shake the drawer and lightly spray with olive oil. Reinsert drawer in unit and press START/PAUSE to resume cooking.
7. When cooking is complete, remove drawer from unit. Transfer prawns to a plate. Serve warm.

Crispy Cod Cakes with Salad Greens

SERVES: 4

PREP TIME: 15 minutes
COOK TIME: 15 minutes

450 g cod fillets, cut into chunks
10 g packed fresh basil leaves
3 cloves garlic, crushed
½ tsp. smoked paprika
¼ tsp. salt
¼ tsp. pepper
1 large egg, beaten
60 g panko bread crumbs
Cooking spray
Salad greens, for serving

1. In a food processor, pulse cod, basil, garlic, smoked paprika, salt, and pepper until cod is finely chopped, stirring occasionally. Form into 8 patties, about 5-cm in diameter. Dip each first into the egg, then into the panko, patting to adhere. Spray with oil on one side.
2. Insert a crisper plate in both drawers. Place 4 cod cakes in a single layer in each drawer, oil-side down; spray with oil.
3. Select Zone 1, select AIR FRY, set temperature to 200°C, and set time to 15 minutes. Select MATCH COOK to match Zone 2 settings to Zone 1. Select START/PAUSE to begin cooking.
4. When cooking is complete, transfer cod cakes to a plate. Serve with salad greens.

Juicy Salmon and Asparagus

SERVES: 2

PREP TIME: 5 minutes
COOK TIME: 18 minutes

2 salmon fillets
4 asparagus stalks
60 ml champagne
Salt and black pepper, to taste
60 ml white sauce
5 ml olive oil

1. Mix all the ingredients in a bowl.
2. Insert a crisper plate in both drawers. Place salmon fillets in the Zone 1 drawer, then insert drawer in unit. Place asparagus stalks in the Zone 2 drawer, then insert drawer in unit.
3. Select Zone 1, select AIR FRY, set temperature to 200°C, and set time to 15 minutes. Select Zone 2, select ROAST, set temperature to 200°C, and set time to 18 minutes. Select SYNC. Press the START/PAUSE button to begin cooking.
4. When the Zone 1 and 2 times reach 8 minutes, press START/PAUSE to pause the unit. Remove the drawers from unit and flip the salmon and asparagus. Reinsert drawers in unit and press START/PAUSE to resume cooking.
5. When cooking is complete, serve salmon with asparagus.

Amazing Salmon Fillets

SERVES: 2

PREP TIME: 5 minutes
COOK TIME: 12 minutes

2 (200 g) (2-cm thick) salmon fillets
1 tbsp. Italian seasoning
15 ml fresh lemon juice

1. Rub the salmon evenly with Italian seasoning.
2. Install a crisper plate in Zone 1 drawer. Place salmon in the drawer, then insert drawer in unit.
3. Select Zone 1, select AIR FRY, set temperature to 200°C, and set time to 12 minutes. Press the START/PAUSE button to begin cooking.
4. When cooking is complete, remove drawer from unit. Transfer salmon to a plate and squeeze lemon juice on it to serve.

Sesame Seeds Coated Tuna with Spinach

SERVES: 2

PREP TIME: 15 minutes
COOK TIME: 15 minutes

40 g white sesame seeds
10 g black sesame seeds
1 egg white
2 (170 g) tuna steaks
1 small onion, chopped
150 g fresh spinach
30 ml olive oil
1 tsp. ginger, minced
Salt and black pepper, to taste

1. Whisk the egg white in a shallow bowl.
2. Mix the sesame seeds, salt, and black pepper in another bowl.
3. Dip the tuna steaks into the whisked egg white and dredge into the sesame seeds mixture.
4. Put olive oil, onions and ginger in a medium bowl.
5. Insert a crisper plate in both drawers. Place tuna steaks in the Zone 1 drawer, then insert drawer in unit. Place onions in the Zone 2 drawer, then insert drawer in unit.
6. Select Zone 1, select AIR FRY, set temperature to 200°C, and set time to 15 minutes. Select Zone 2, select AIR FRY, set temperature to 200°C, and set time to 12 minutes. Select SYNC. Press the START/PAUSE button to begin cooking.
7. When the Zone 1 and 2 times reach 6 minutes, press START/PAUSE to pause the unit. Remove the drawers from unit and flip the tuna steaks over. Add spinach, salt, and black pepper in the Zone 2 drawer. Reinsert drawers in unit and press START/PAUSE to resume cooking.
8. When cooking is complete, serve tuna steaks with vegetables.

Ranch Tilapia

SERVES: 4

PREP TIME: 15 minutes
COOK TIME: 15 minutes

65 g cornflakes, crushed
2 eggs
4 (170 g) tilapia fillets
37 ml vegetable oil
For Ranch Dressing:
60 g dry buttermilk powder
1 tbsp. dried parsley
2 tsps. dried dill
1 tsp. freeze dried chives
1 tbsp. garlic powder
1 tbsp. onion powder
1 tsp. sea salt
½ tsp. ground black pepper

1. Whisk the eggs in a shallow bowl.
2. Mix cornflakes, ranch dressing and olive oil in another bowl until a crumbly mixture is formed.
3. Dip the tilapia fillets into whisked eggs and dredge into the breadcrumb mixture.
4. Insert a crisper plate in both drawers. Place 2 tilapia fillets in a single layer in each drawer.
5. Select Zone 1, select AIR FRY, set temperature to 200°C, and set time to 15 minutes. Select MATCH COOK to match Zone 2 settings to Zone 1. Select START/PAUSE to begin cooking.
6. When the Zone 1 and 2 times reach 8 minutes, press START/PAUSE to pause the unit. Remove the drawers from unit and flip the tilapia fillets over. Lightly spray with the cooking spray. Reinsert drawers in unit and press START/PAUSE to resume cooking.
7. When cooking is complete, transfer tilapia fillets to a plate. Serve warm.

Southern Style Catfish

SERVES: 6

PREP TIME: 15 minutes
COOK TIME: 15 minutes

6 (170 g) catfish fillets
240 ml milk
60 g cornmeal
30 g plain flour
Olive oil cooking spray
10 ml fresh lemon juice
120 ml yellow mustard
2 tbsps. dried parsley flakes
¼ tsp. red chilli powder
¼ tsp. cayenne pepper
¼ tsp. onion powder
¼ tsp. garlic powder
Salt and ground black pepper, as required

1. Mix catfish, milk, and lemon juice in a large bowl and refrigerate for about 30 minutes.
2. Put the mustard in a shallow bowl and mix the cornmeal, flour, parsley flakes, and spices in another bowl.
3. Remove the catfish fillets from milk mixture and coat each fish fillet with mustard. Roll evenly into the cornmeal mixture.
4. Insert a crisper plate in both drawers. Place 3 catfish fillets in a single layer in each drawer. Spray with the olive oil cooking spray.
5. Select Zone 1, select AIR FRY, set temperature to 200°C, and set time to 15 minutes. Select MATCH COOK to match Zone 2 settings to Zone 1. Select START/PAUSE to begin cooking.
6. When the Zone 1 and 2 times reach 8 minutes, press START/PAUSE to pause the unit. Remove the drawers from unit and flip the catfish fillets over. Lightly spray with the cooking spray. Reinsert drawers in unit and press START/PAUSE to resume cooking.
7. When cooking is complete, transfer catfish fillets to a plate. Serve warm.

Crispy Cod Sticks

SERVES: 2

PREP TIME: 20 minutes
COOK TIME: 10 minutes

3 (115 g) skinless cod fillets, cut into rectangular pieces
95 g flour
4 eggs
1 green chilli, finely chopped
2 garlic cloves, minced
10 ml light soy sauce
Salt and ground black pepper, to taste

1. Place flour in a shallow dish and whisk the eggs, garlic, green chilli, soy sauce, salt, and black pepper in a second dish.
2. Coat the cod fillets evenly in flour and dip in the egg mixture.
3. Install a crisper plate in Zone 1 drawer. Place cod pieces in the drawer, then insert drawer in unit.
4. Select Zone 1, select AIR FRY, set temperature to 200°C, and set time to 10 minutes. Press the START/PAUSE button to begin cooking.
5. When cooking is complete, remove drawer from unit. Transfer cod pieces to a plate. Serve warm.

Cod with Prawns and Pasta

SERVES: 4

PREP TIME: 20 minutes
COOK TIME: 25 minutes

400 g pasta
4 (115 g) cod steaks
8 large prawns, peeled and deveined
6 g fresh parsley, chopped
4 tbsps. pesto
30 ml olive oil
30 ml fresh lemon juice

1. Cook pasta in a large pan of salted water for about 10 minutes.
2. Meanwhile, spread pesto over cod steaks and drizzle evenly with olive oil.
3. Sprinkle prawns with lemon juice and parsley.
4. Insert a crisper plate in both drawers. Place cod steaks in the Zone 1 drawer, then insert drawer in unit. Place prawns in the Zone 2 drawer, then insert drawer in unit.
5. Select Zone 1, select AIR FRY, set temperature to 200°C, and set time to 15 minutes. Select Zone 2, select AIR FRY, set temperature to 200°C, and set time to 13 minutes. Select SYNC. Press the START/PAUSE button to begin cooking.
6. When cooking is complete, serve the cod with prawns and pasta.

CHAPTER 5
VEGETABLES

Lemony Green Beans 36
Stuffed Okra 36
Parmesan Asparagus 37
Caramelised Brussels Sprouts 37
Potato Salad 38
Crispy Bacon-Wrapped Asparagus Bundles 38
Buttered Broccoli 39
Garden Fresh Green Beans 39
Ritzy Vegetable Frittata 40
Spiced Aubergine 40
Aubergine Salad 41
Veggie-filled Pumpkin Basket 41

Lemony Green Beans

SERVES: 3

PREP TIME: 15 minutes
COOK TIME: 12 minutes

450 g green beans, trimmed and halved
15 ml fresh lemon juice
5 g unsalted butter, melted
¼ tsp. garlic powder

1. Mix all the ingredients in a bowl and toss to coat well.
2. Install a crisper plate in Zone 1 drawer. Place green beans in the drawer, then insert drawer in unit.
3. Select Zone 1, select AIR FRY, set temperature to 200°C, and set time to 12 minutes. Press the START/PAUSE button to begin cooking.
4. With 5 minutes remaining, press START/PAUSE to pause the unit. Remove the drawer from unit and flip the green beans over. Reinsert drawer in unit and press START/PAUSE to resume cooking.
5. When cooking is complete, remove drawer from unit. Transfer green beans to a plate. Serve warm.

Stuffed Okra

SERVES: 2

PREP TIME: 15 minutes
COOK TIME: 12 minutes

225 g large okras
30 g chickpea flour
¼ of onion, chopped
15 g coconut, grated freshly
1 tsp. garam masala powder
½ tsp. ground turmeric
½ tsp. red chilli powder
½ tsp. ground cumin
Salt, to taste

1. Mix the flour, onion, grated coconut, and spices in a bowl and toss to coat well.
2. Install a crisper plate in Zone 1 drawer. Stuff the flour mixture into okras and arrange in the drawer, then insert drawer in unit.
3. Select Zone 1, select AIR FRY, set temperature to 200°C, and set time to 12 minutes. Press the START/PAUSE button to begin cooking.
4. With 6 minutes remaining, press START/PAUSE to pause the unit. Remove the drawer from unit and flip the okras over. Reinsert drawer in unit and press START/PAUSE to resume cooking.
5. When cooking is complete, remove drawer from unit. Transfer okras to a plate. Serve warm.

Parmesan Asparagus

SERVES: 3

PREP TIME: 15 minutes
COOK TIME: 20 minutes

450 g fresh asparagus, trimmed
15 g Parmesan cheese, grated
15 g butter, melted
1 tsp. garlic powder
Salt and black pepper, to taste

1. Mix the asparagus, cheese, butter, garlic powder, salt, and black pepper in a bowl and toss to coat well.
2. Install a crisper plate in Zone 1 drawer. Place asparagus in the drawer, then insert drawer in unit.
3. Select Zone 1, select ROAST, set temperature to 200°C, and set time to 20 minutes. Press the START/PAUSE button to begin cooking.
4. With 10 minutes remaining, press START/PAUSE to pause the unit. Remove the drawer from unit and shake for 10 seconds. Reinsert drawer in unit and press START/PAUSE to resume cooking.
5. When cooking is complete, remove drawer from unit. Transfer asparagus to a plate. Serve warm.

Caramelised Brussels Sprouts

SERVES: 4

PREP TIME: 10 minutes
COOK TIME: 20 minutes

450 g Brussels sprouts, trimmed and halved
20 g butter, melted
Salt and black pepper, to taste

1. Mix all the ingredients in a bowl and toss to coat well.
2. Install a crisper plate in Zone 1 drawer. Place Brussels sprouts in the drawer, then insert drawer in unit.
3. Select Zone 1, select AIR FRY, set temperature to 200°C, and set time to 20 minutes. Press the START/PAUSE button to begin cooking.
4. With 10 minutes remaining, press START/PAUSE to pause the unit. Remove the drawer from unit and flip the Brussels sprouts over. Reinsert drawer in unit and press START/PAUSE to resume cooking.
5. When cooking is complete, remove drawer from unit. Transfer Brussels sprouts to a plate. Serve warm.

Potato Salad

SERVES: 5

PREP TIME: 10 minutes
COOK TIME: 30 minutes

4 Russet potatoes
3 hard-boiled eggs, peeled and chopped
100 g celery, chopped
80 g red onion, chopped
15 ml olive oil
Salt, as required
15 ml prepared mustard
¼ tsp. celery salt
¼ tsp. garlic salt
60 ml mayonnaise

1. Prick the potatoes with a fork and rub with olive oil and salt.
2. Install a crisper plate in Zone 1 drawer. Place potatoes in the drawer, then insert drawer in unit.
3. Select Zone 1, select ROAST, set temperature to 200°C, and set time to 30 minutes. Press the START/PAUSE button to begin cooking.
4. When cooking is complete, remove drawer from unit. Transfer potatoes to a plate and keep aside to cool.
5. Add the remaining ingredients and mix well.
6. Refrigerate for about 2 hours and serve immediately.

Crispy Bacon-Wrapped Asparagus Bundles

SERVES: 4

PREP TIME: 20 minutes
COOK TIME: 12 minutes

450 g asparagus
4 rashers of bacon
5 g sesame seeds, toasted
1 garlic clove, minced
22 g brown sugar
12 ml olive oil
7 ml sesame oil

1. Mix garlic, brown sugar, olive oil and sesame oil in a bowl till sugar is dissolved.
2. Divide asparagus into 4 equal bunches and wrap a rasher of bacon around each bunch.
3. Rub the asparagus bunch with garlic mixture.
4. Install a crisper plate in Zone 1 drawer. Place asparagus bunches in the drawer and sprinkle with sesame seeds, then insert drawer in unit.
5. Select Zone 1, select ROAST, set temperature to 200°C, and set time to 12 minutes. Press the START/PAUSE button to begin cooking.
6. With 6 minutes remaining, press START/PAUSE to pause the unit. Remove the drawer from unit and flip the asparagus bunches over. Reinsert drawer in unit and press START/PAUSE to resume cooking.
7. When cooking is complete, remove drawer from unit. Transfer asparagus bunches to a plate. Serve warm.

Buttered Broccoli

SERVES: 4

PREP TIME: 10 minutes
COOK TIME: 10 minutes

480 g fresh broccoli florets
30 g butter, melted
Salt and black pepper, to taste

1. Mix broccoli, butter, salt, and black pepper in a bowl and toss to coat well.
2. Install a crisper plate in Zone 1 drawer. Place broccoli florets in the drawer, then insert drawer in unit.
3. Select Zone 1, select AIR FRY, set temperature to 200°C, and set time to 10 minutes. Press the START/PAUSE button to begin cooking.
4. With 5 minutes remaining, press START/PAUSE to pause the unit. Remove the drawer from unit and flip the broccoli florets over. Reinsert drawer in unit and press START/PAUSE to resume cooking.
5. When cooking is complete, remove drawer from unit. Transfer broccoli florets to a plate. Serve warm.

Garden Fresh Green Beans

SERVES: 4

PREP TIME: 10 minutes
COOK TIME: 12 minutes

cooking spray
450 g green beans, washed and trimmed
5 g butter, melted
15 ml fresh lemon juice
¼ tsp. garlic powder
Salt and freshly ground pepper, to taste

1. Put all the ingredients in a large bowl.
2. Install a crisper plate in Zone 1 drawer. Place green beans in the drawer and spray with cooking spray, then insert drawer in unit.
3. Select Zone 1, select AIR FRY, set temperature to 200°C, and set time to 12 minutes. Press the START/PAUSE button to begin cooking.
4. With 6 minutes remaining, press START/PAUSE to pause the unit. Remove the drawer from unit and flip the green beans over. Reinsert drawer in unit and press START/PAUSE to resume cooking.
5. When cooking is complete, remove drawer from unit. Transfer green beans to a plate. Serve warm.

Ritzy Vegetable Frittata

SERVES: 2

PREP TIME: 15 minutes
COOK TIME: 24 minutes

4 eggs
60 ml milk
Sea salt and ground black pepper, to taste
1 courgette, sliced
½ bunch asparagus, sliced
60 g mushrooms, sliced
30 g spinach, shredded
80 g red onion, sliced
7 ml olive oil
75 g feta cheese, crumbled
40 g Cheddar cheese, grated
¼ bunch chives, minced

1. In a bowl, mix the eggs, milk, salt and pepper.
2. Over a medium heat, sauté the vegetables for 6 minutes with the olive oil in a nonstick pan.
3. Pour in the vegetables into two 13-cm cake pan followed by the egg mixture. Top with the feta and grated Cheddar.
4. Insert a crisper plate in both drawers. Place one cake pan in each drawer.
5. Select Zone 1, select BAKE, set temperature to 160°C, and set time to 18 minutes. Select MATCH COOK to match Zone 2 settings to Zone 1. Select START/PAUSE to begin cooking.
6. When cooking is complete, transfer cake pans to a plate and leave to cool for 5 minutes. Top with the minced chives and serve.

Spiced Aubergine

SERVES: 3

PREP TIME: 15 minutes
COOK TIME: 15 minutes

2 medium aubergines, cubed
30 g butter, melted
30 g Parmesan cheese, shredded
15 ml Maggi seasoning sauce
1 tsp. sumac
1 tsp. garlic powder
1 tsp. onion powder
Salt and ground black pepper, as required
15 ml fresh lemon juice

1. Mix the aubergine cubes, butter, seasoning sauce and spices in a bowl and toss to coat well.
2. Install a crisper plate in Zone 1 drawer. Place aubergine cubes in the drawer, then insert drawer in unit.
3. Select Zone 1, select AIR FRY, set temperature to 200°C, and set time to 15 minutes. Press the START/PAUSE button to begin cooking.
4. With 8 minutes remaining, press START/PAUSE to pause the unit. Remove the drawer from unit and shake for 10 seconds. Reinsert drawer in unit and press START/PAUSE to resume cooking.
5. When cooking is complete, remove drawer from unit. Transfer aubergine cubes to a plate and sprinkle with lemon juice and Parmesan cheese to serve.

Aubergine Salad

SERVES: 2

PREP TIME: 15 minutes
COOK TIME: 15 minutes

1 aubergine, cut into 1-cm-thick slices crosswise
1 avocado, peeled, pitted and chopped
30 ml rapeseed oil
Salt and ground black pepper, as required
5 ml fresh lemon juice
For the Dressing:
15 ml extra-virgin olive oil
15 ml red wine vinegar
15 ml honey
15 ml fresh oregano leaves, chopped
1 tsp. fresh lemon zest, grated
1 tsp. Dijon mustard
Salt and ground black pepper, as required

1. Mix aubergine, oil, salt, and black pepper in a bowl and toss to coat well.
2. Install a crisper plate in Zone 1 drawer. Place aubergines pieces in the drawer, then insert drawer in unit.
3. Select Zone 1, select AIR FRY, set temperature to 200°C, and set time to 15 minutes. Press the START/PAUSE button to begin cooking.
4. With 8 minutes remaining, press START/PAUSE to pause the unit. Remove the drawer from unit and flip the aubergines pieces over. Reinsert drawer in unit and press START/PAUSE to resume cooking.
5. When cooking is complete, remove drawer from unit. Transfer aubergines to a plate and keep aside to cool.
6. Add avocado and lemon juice and mix well.
7. Mix all the ingredients for dressing in a bowl and pour over the salad.
8. Toss to coat well and serve immediately.

Veggie-filled Pumpkin Basket

SERVES: 6

PREP TIME: 15 minutes
COOK TIME: 30 minutes

1 sweet potato, peeled and chopped
1 parsnip, peeled and chopped
120 g peas, shelled
1 onion, chopped
1 pumpkin, seeded and halved
2 garlic cloves, minced
2 tsps. herb mix

1. Mix all the ingredients in a bowl except pumpkin and toss to coat well.
2. Stuff half of the vegetable mixture into pumpkin halves.
3. Insert a crisper plate in both drawers. Place the pumpkin halve in each drawer.
4. Select Zone 1, select ROAST, set temperature to 200°C, and set time to 30 minutes. Select MATCH COOK to match Zone 2 settings to Zone 1. Select START/PAUSE to begin cooking.
5. unit and press START/PAUSE to resume cooking.
6. When cooking is complete, transfer pumpkin halves to a plate. Serve warm.

CHAPTER 6
PORK

BBQ Pork Steaks 43
Marinated Pork Tenderloin 43
Bacon Wrapped Pork Tenderloin 44
Easy Devils on Horseback 44
Smoky Flavoured Pork Ribs 45
Barbecue Pork Ribs with Green Beans 45
Bacon-Wrapped Jalapeño Poppers 46
Air Fried Pork Loin Back Ribs 46
Vietnamese Pork Chops 47
Pork Tenderloin with Bell Peppers 47
Ham Pinwheels 48
Pork Tenderloin with Bacon and Veggies 48

BBQ Pork Steaks

SERVES: 4

PREP TIME: 5 minutes
COOK TIME: 17 minutes

4 pork steaks
14 g Cajun seasoning
30 ml BBQ sauce
15 ml vinegar
5 ml soy sauce
100 g brown sugar
120 ml ketchup

1. Sprinkle pork steaks with Cajun seasoning.
2. Combine remaining ingredients and brush onto steaks.
3. Insert a crisper plate in both drawers. Place 2 steaks in a single layer in each drawer.
4. Select Zone 1, select AIR FRY, set temperature to 190°C, and set time to 17 minutes. Select MATCH COOK to match Zone 2 settings to Zone 1. Select START/PAUSE to begin cooking.
5. When the Zone 1 and 2 times reach 8 minutes, press START/PAUSE to pause the unit. Remove the drawers from unit and flip the steaks over. Reinsert drawers in unit and press START/PAUSE to resume cooking.
6. When cooking is complete, transfer steaks to a plate. Serve warm.

Marinated Pork Tenderloin

SERVES : 4 TO 6

PREP TIME: 10 minutes
COOK TIME: 30 minutes

60 ml olive oil
60 ml soy sauce
60 ml freshly squeezed lemon juice
1 garlic clove, minced
15 g Dijon mustard
1 tsp. salt
½ tsp. freshly ground black pepper
900 g pork tenderloin

1. In a large mixing bowl, make the marinade: Mix the olive oil, soy sauce, lemon juice, minced garlic, Dijon mustard, salt, and pepper. Reserve 60 ml of the marinade.
2. Put the tenderloin in a large bowl and pour the remaining marinade over the meat. Cover and marinate in the refrigerator for about 1 hour.
3. Install a crisper plate in Zone 1 drawer. Place marinated pork tenderloin in the drawer, then insert drawer in unit.
4. Select Zone 1, select ROAST, set temperature to 190°C, and set time to 30 minutes. Press the START/PAUSE button to begin cooking.
5. With 20 minutes remaining, press START/PAUSE to pause the unit. Remove the drawer from unit. Flip the pork over and baste it with half of the reserved marinade. Reinsert drawer in unit and press START/PAUSE to resume cooking.
6. With 10 minutes remaining, press START/PAUSE to pause the unit. Remove the drawer from unit. Flip the pork over and baste it with the remaining marinade. Reinsert drawer in unit and press START/PAUSE to resume cooking.
7. When cooking is complete, remove drawer from unit. Allow to sit 8 minutes to rest before slicing.

Bacon Wrapped Pork Tenderloin

SERVES: 4

PREP TIME: 15 minutes
COOK TIME: 30 minutes

1 (680 g) pork tenderloins
4 rashers of bacon
30 g Dijon mustard

1. Rub the tenderloin evenly with mustard and wrap the tenderloin with rashers of bacon.
2. Install a crisper plate in Zone 1 drawer. Place pork tenderloin in the drawer, then insert drawer in unit.
3. Select Zone 1, select ROAST, set temperature to 190°C, and set time to 30 minutes. Press the START/PAUSE button to begin cooking.
4. With 15 minutes remaining, press START/PAUSE to pause the unit. Remove the drawer from unit and flip the pork tenderloin over. Re-insert drawer in unit and press START/PAUSE to resume cooking.
5. When cooking is complete, remove drawer from unit. Transfer pork tenderloin to a plate. Cut into desired size slices to serve.

Easy Devils on Horseback

SERVES: 12

PREP TIME: 5 minutes
COOK TIME: 12 minutes

24 (about 130 g) petite pitted prunes
30 g crumbled blue stilton cheese, divided
8 rashers of middle bacon, cut crosswise into thirds

1. Halve the prunes lengthwise, but don't cut them all the way through. Place ½ tsp. of cheese in the centre of each prune. Wrap a piece of bacon around each prune and secure the bacon with a toothpick.
2. Insert a crisper plate in both drawers. Place half of the prunes in a single layer in each drawer.
3. Select Zone 1, select AIR FRY, set temperature to 200°C, and set time to 12 minutes. Select MATCH COOK to match Zone 2 settings to Zone 1. Select START/PAUSE to begin cooking.
4. When the Zone 1 and 2 times reach 6 minutes, press START/PAUSE to pause the unit. Remove the drawers from unit and flip the prunes over. Reinsert drawers in unit and press START/PAUSE to resume cooking.
5. When cooking is complete, transfer prunes to a plate. Serve warm.

Smoky Flavoured Pork Ribs

SERVES: 6

PREP TIME: 10 minutes
COOK TIME: 18 minutes

800 g pork ribs
60 ml honey, divided
180 ml BBQ sauce
30 ml tomato ketchup
15 ml Worcestershire sauce
15 ml soy sauce
½ tsp. garlic powder
Freshly ground white pepper, to taste

1. Mix 3 tbsps. of honey and remaining ingredients in a large bowl except the ribs.
2. Coat the pork ribs with marinade generously and cover to refrigerate for about 30 minutes.
3. Install a crisper plate in Zone 1 drawer. Place ribs in the drawer, then insert drawer in unit.
4. Select Zone 1, select AIR FRY, set temperature to 180°C, and set time to 18 minutes. Press the START/PAUSE button to begin cooking.
5. With 8 minutes remaining, press START/PAUSE to pause the unit. Remove the drawer from unit and flip the ribs over. Reinsert drawer in unit and press START/PAUSE to resume cooking.
6. When cooking is complete, remove drawer from unit. Transfer ribs to a plate. Coat with remaining honey and serve hot.

Barbecue Pork Ribs with Green Beans

SERVES: 4

PREP TIME: 5 minutes
COOK TIME: 30 minutes

1 tbsp. barbecue dry rub
5 g mustard
15 ml apple cider vinegar
5 ml sesame oil
450 g pork ribs, chopped
450 g green beans, trimmed and halved
5 g unsalted butter, melted
¼ tsp. garlic powder

1. Combine the dry rub, mustard, apple cider vinegar, and sesame oil, then coat the ribs with this mixture. Refrigerate the ribs for 20 minutes.
2. Mix green beans, butter and garlic powder in a bowl and toss to coat well.
3. Insert a crisper plate in both drawers. Place ribs in the Zone 1 drawer, then insert drawer in unit. Place green beans in the Zone 2 drawer, then insert drawer in unit.
4. Select Zone 1, select AIR FRY, set temperature to 190°C, and set time to 30 minutes. Select Zone 2, select AIR FRY, set temperature to 200°C, and set time to 15 minutes. Select SYNC. Press the START/PAUSE button to begin cooking.
5. When the Zone 1 and Zone 2 times reach 10 minutes, press START/PAUSE and remove drawers from unit. In Zone 1, flip the rib over. In Zone 2, shake for 10 seconds. Reinsert drawers in unit and press START/PAUSE to resume cooking.
6. When cooking is complete, serve rib with green beans.

Bacon-Wrapped Jalapeño Poppers

SERVES: 6

PREP TIME: 5 minutes
COOK TIME: 16 minutes

6 large jalapeños
115 g ⅓-less-fat cream cheese
30 g shredded reduced-fat sharp Cheddar cheese
2 spring onions, green tops only, sliced
6 rashers of middle bacon, halved

1. Wearing rubber gloves, halve the jalapeños lengthwise to make 12 pieces. Scoop out the seeds and membranes and discard.
2. In a medium bowl, combine the cream cheese, Cheddar, and spring onions. Using a small spoon or spatula, fill the jalapeños with the cream cheese filling. Wrap a rasher of bacon around each pepper and secure with a toothpick.
3. Insert a crisper plate in both drawers. Place half of stuffed peppers in a single layer in each drawer.
4. Select Zone 1, select AIR FRY, set temperature to 200°C, and set time to 16 minutes. Select MATCH COOK to match Zone 2 settings to Zone 1. Select START/PAUSE to begin cooking, until the peppers are tender, the bacon is browned and crisp, and the cheese is melted.
5. When cooking is complete, transfer stuffed peppers to a plate. Serve warm.

Air Fried Pork Loin Back Ribs

SERVES: 2

PREP TIME: 5 minutes
COOK TIME: 30 minutes

2 tsps. red pepper flakes
¾ tsp. ground ginger
3 cloves minced garlic
Salt and ground black pepper, to taste
2 pork loin back ribs

1. Combine the red pepper flakes, ginger, garlic, salt and pepper in a bowl, making sure to mix well. Massage the mixture into the pork loin back ribs.
2. Install a crisper plate in Zone 1 drawer. Place pork loin back ribs in the drawer, then insert drawer in unit.
3. Select Zone 1, select AIR FRY, set temperature to 190°C, and set time to 30 minutes. Press the START/PAUSE button to begin cooking.
4. With 15 minutes remaining, press START/PAUSE to pause the unit. Remove the drawer from unit and flip the pork loin back ribs over. Reinsert drawer in unit and press START/PAUSE to resume cooking.
5. When cooking is complete, remove drawer from unit. Transfer pork loin back ribs to a plate. Serve warm.

Vietnamese Pork Chops

SERVES: 2

PREP TIME: 15 minutes
COOK TIME: 15 minutes

10 g chopped shallot
9 g chopped garlic
15 ml fish sauce
15 g lemongrass
5 ml soy sauce
12 g brown sugar
15 ml olive oil
1 tsp. ground black pepper
2 pork chops

1. Combine shallot, garlic, fish sauce, lemongrass, soy sauce, brown sugar, olive oil, and pepper in a bowl. Stir to mix well.
2. Put the pork chops in the bowl. Toss to coat well. Place the bowl in the refrigerator to marinate for 2 hours.
3. Remove the pork chops from the bowl and discard the marinade. Install a crisper plate in Zone 1 drawer. Place pork chops in the drawer, then insert drawer in unit.
4. Select Zone 1, select AIR FRY, set temperature to 190°C, and set time to 15 minutes. Press the START/PAUSE button to begin cooking.
5. With 8 minutes remaining, press START/PAUSE to pause the unit. Remove the drawer from unit and flip the pork chops over. Reinsert drawer in unit and press START/PAUSE to resume cooking.
6. When cooking is complete, remove drawer from unit. Transfer pork chops to a plate. Serve warm.

Pork Tenderloin with Bell Peppers

SERVES: 3

PREP TIME: 20 minutes
COOK TIME: 22 minutes

1 large red bell pepper, seeded and cut into thin strips
1 red onion, thinly sliced
310 g pork tenderloin, cut into 4 pieces
2 tsps. Herbs de Provence
Salt and ground black pepper, as required
15 ml olive oil
½ tbsp. Dijon mustard

1. Mix the bell pepper, onion, Herbs de Provence, salt, black pepper, and 7 ml oil in a bowl.
2. Rub the tenderloin evenly with mustard, salt, and black pepper and drizzle with the remaining oil.
3. Insert a crisper plate in both drawers. Place bell pepper mixture in the Zone 1 drawer, then insert drawer in unit. Place pork tenderloin in the Zone 2 drawer, then insert drawer in unit.
4. Select Zone 1, select ROAST, set temperature to 200°C, and set time to 15 minutes. Select Zone 2, select AIR FRY, set temperature to 190°C, and set time to 22 minutes. Select SYNC. Press the START/PAUSE button to begin cooking.
5. When the Zone 1 and 2 times reach 8 minutes, press START/PAUSE to pause the unit. Remove the drawers from unit and flip the tenderloin and bell pepper mixture over. Reinsert drawers in unit and press START/PAUSE to resume cooking.
6. When cooking is complete, dish out the tenderloin and cut into desired size slices. Serve with bell pepper.

Ham Pinwheels

SERVES: 4

PREP TIME: 15 minutes
COOK TIME: 12 minutes

1 puff pastry sheet
10 ham slices
120 g Gruyere cheese, shredded plus more for sprinkling
20 g Dijon mustard

1. Place the puff pastry onto a smooth surface and spread evenly with the mustard.
2. Top with the ham and 90 g cheese and roll the puff pastry.
3. Wrap the roll in clingfilm and freeze for about 30 minutes.
4. Remove from the freezer and slice into 1-cm rounds.
5. Install a crisper plate in Zone 1 drawer. Place pinwheels in the drawer, then insert drawer in unit.
6. Select Zone 1, select BAKE, set temperature to 190°C, and set time to 12 minutes. Press the START/PAUSE button to begin cooking.
7. With 6 minutes remaining, press START/PAUSE to pause the unit. Remove the drawer from unit and top with remaining cheese. Reinsert drawer in unit and press START/PAUSE to resume cooking.
8. When cooking is complete, remove drawer from unit. Transfer pinwheels to a plate. Serve warm.

Pork Tenderloin with Bacon and Veggies

SERVES: 3

PREP TIME: 20 minutes
COOK TIME: 40 minutes

3 potatoes
340 g frozen green beans
6 rashers of bacon
3 (170 g) pork tenderloins
30 ml olive oil

1. Pierce the potatoes with a fork.
2. Wrap 4-6 green beans with one rasher of bacon and coat the pork tenderloins with olive oil.
3. Insert a crisper plate in both drawers. Place potatoes in the Zone 1 drawer, then insert drawer in unit. Place pork tenderloins in the Zone 2 drawer, then insert drawer in unit.
4. Select Zone 1, select ROAST, set temperature to 200°C, and set time to 40 minutes. Select Zone 2, select AIR FRY, set temperature to 190°C, and set time to 25 minutes. Press the START/PAUSE button to begin cooking.
5. When the Zone 2 time reaches zero, gently transfer pork tenderloins to a serving dish and cut into desired size slices.
6. Arrange the bean rolls in the Zone 2 drawer, then insert drawer in unit. Select Zone 2, select AIR FRY, set temperature to 200°C, and set time to 15 minutes.
7. When cooking is complete, transfer potatoes and bean rolls to a plate. Then preheat the pork tenderloins. Serve warm.

CHAPTER 7
LAMB

Herbed Lamb Chops ········· 50
Garlicky Lamb Chops ········· 50
Mustard Lamb Loin Chops ········· 51
Nut Crusted Rack of Lamb ········· 51
Lamb Meatballs ········· 52
Fantastic Leg of Lamb ········· 52
Spicy Lamb Kebabs ········· 53
Lamb with Potatoes ········· 53
Italian Lamb Chops with Avocado Mayo ········· 54
Spiced Lamb Steaks ········· 54
Roasted Lamb ········· 55
Greek Lamb Pitta Pockets ········· 55

Herbed Lamb Chops

SERVES: 2

PREP TIME: 10 minutes
COOK TIME: 15 minutes

4 (115 g) lamb chops
15 ml fresh lemon juice
15 ml olive oil
1 tsp. dried rosemary
1 tsp. dried thyme
1 tsp. dried oregano
½ tsp. ground cumin
½ tsp. ground coriander
Salt and black pepper, to taste

1. Mix the lemon juice, oil, herbs, and spices in a large bowl.
2. Coat the chops generously with the herb mixture and refrigerate to marinate for about 1 hour.
3. Install a crisper plate in Zone 1 drawer. Place chops in the drawer, then insert drawer in unit.
4. Select Zone 1, select AIR FRY, set temperature to 200°C, and set time to 15 minutes. Press the START/PAUSE button to begin cooking.
5. With 7 minutes remaining, press START/PAUSE to pause the unit. Remove the drawer from unit and flip the chops over. Reinsert drawer in unit and press START/PAUSE to resume cooking.
6. When cooking is complete, remove drawer from unit. Transfer chops to a plate. Serve warm.

Garlicky Lamb Chops

SERVES: 2

PREP TIME: 20 minutes
COOK TIME: 17 minutes

3 g fresh oregano, chopped
4 g fresh thyme, chopped
8 (115 g) lamb chops
60 ml olive oil, divided
1 bulb garlic, halved
Salt and black pepper, to taste

1. Rub the garlic bulb halves with about 30 ml of the olive oil.
2. Mix remaining oil, herbs, salt and black pepper in a large bowl. Coat the lamb chops with about 1 tbsp. of the herb mixture.
3. Insert a crisper plate in both drawers. Place 4 lamb chops and garlic bulb halve in a single layer in each drawer.
4. Select Zone 1, select ROAST, set temperature to 200°C, and set time to 17 minutes. Select MATCH COOK to match Zone 2 settings to Zone 1. Select START/PAUSE to begin cooking.
5. When the Zone 1 and 2 times reach 8 minutes, press START/PAUSE to pause the unit. Remove the drawers from unit and flip the lamb chops over. Reinsert drawers in unit and press START/PAUSE to resume cooking.
6. When cooking is complete, transfer lamb chops to a plate and serve with herb mixture.

Mustard Lamb Loin Chops

SERVES: 4

PREP TIME: 15 minutes
COOK TIME: 18 minutes

8 (115 g) lamb loin chops
30 g Dijon mustard
15 ml fresh lemon juice
7 ml olive oil
1 tsp. dried tarragon
Salt and black pepper, to taste

1. Mix the mustard, lemon juice, oil, tarragon, salt, and black pepper in a large bowl.
2. Coat the chops generously with the mustard mixture.
3. Insert a crisper plate in both drawers. Place 4 chops in a single layer in each drawer.
4. Select Zone 1, select ROAST, set temperature to 200°C, and set time to 18 minutes. Select MATCH COOK to match Zone 2 settings to Zone 1. Select START/PAUSE to begin cooking.
5. When the Zone 1 and 2 times reach 8 minutes, press START/PAUSE to pause the unit. Remove the drawers from unit and flip the chops over. Reinsert drawers in unit and press START/PAUSE to resume cooking.
6. When cooking is complete, transfer chops to a plate. Serve warm.

Nut Crusted Rack of Lamb

SERVES: 6

PREP TIME: 15 minutes
COOK TIME: 35 minutes

800 g rack of lamb
1 egg
6 g breadcrumbs
85 g almonds, chopped finely
2 g fresh rosemary, chopped
15 ml olive oil
1 garlic clove, minced
Salt and black pepper, to taste

1. Mix garlic, olive oil, salt and black pepper in a bowl.
2. Whisk the egg in a shallow dish and mix breadcrumbs, almonds and rosemary in another shallow dish.
3. Coat the rack of lamb with garlic mixture evenly, dip into the egg and dredge into the breadcrumb mixture.
4. Install a crisper plate in Zone 1 drawer. Place rack of lamb in the drawer, then insert drawer in unit.
5. Select Zone 1, select ROAST, set temperature to 200°C, and set time to 35 minutes. Press the START/PAUSE button to begin cooking.
6. With 15 minutes remaining, press START/PAUSE to pause the unit. Remove the drawer from unit and flip the rack of lamb over. Reinsert drawer in unit and press START/PAUSE to resume cooking.
7. When cooking is complete, remove drawer from unit. Transfer the rack of lamb to a plate. Serve warm.

Lamb Meatballs

SERVES: 4

PREP TIME: 20 minutes
COOK TIME: 27 minutes

For the Meatballs:
½ small onion, finely diced
1 clove garlic, minced
450 g minced lamb
5 g fresh parsley, finely chopped (plus more for garnish)
2 tsps. fresh oregano, finely chopped
30 ml milk
1 egg yolk
Salt and freshly ground black pepper, to taste
60 g crumbled feta cheese, for garnish

For the Tomato Sauce:
30 g butter
1 clove garlic, smashed
Pinch crushed red pepper flakes
¼ tsp. ground cinnamon
1 (800 g) tin crushed tomatoes
Salt, to taste
Cooking spray

1. Combine all ingredients for the meatballs in a large bowl and mix just until everything is combined. Shape the mixture into 4-cm balls or shape the meat between two spoons to make quenelles.
2. Start the quick tomato sauce. Put the butter, garlic and red pepper flakes in a sauté pan and heat over medium heat on the hob. Let the garlic sizzle a little, but before the butter browns, add the cinnamon and tomatoes. Bring to a simmer and simmer for 15 minutes. Season with salt.
3. Insert a crisper plate in both drawers. Place half of the meatballs in a single layer in each drawer. Spray with cooking spray.
4. Select Zone 1, select AIR FRY, set temperature to 200°C, and set time to 12 minutes. Select MATCH COOK to match Zone 2 settings to Zone 1. Select START/PAUSE to begin cooking.
5. When the Zone 1 and 2 times reach 6 minutes, press START/PAUSE to pause the unit. Remove the drawers from unit and flip the meatballs over. Reinsert drawers in unit and press START/PAUSE to resume cooking.
6. When cooking is complete, transfer meatballs to a plate. To serve, spoon a pool of the tomato sauce onto plates and add the meatballs. Sprinkle the feta cheese on top and garnish with more fresh parsley. Serve immediately.

Fantastic Leg of Lamb

SERVES: 4

PREP TIME: 10 minutes
COOK TIME: 50 minutes

900 g leg of lamb
2 fresh rosemary sprigs
2 fresh thyme sprigs
30 ml olive oil
Salt and black pepper, to taste

1. Sprinkle the leg of lamb with oil, salt and black pepper and wrap with herb sprigs.
2. Install a crisper plate in Zone 1 drawer. Place leg of lamb in the drawer, then insert drawer in unit.
3. Select Zone 1, select ROAST, set temperature to 200°C, and set time to 50 minutes. Press the START/PAUSE button to begin cooking.
4. With 25 minutes remaining, press START/PAUSE to pause the unit. Remove the drawer from unit and flip the leg of lamb over. Reinsert drawer in unit and press START/PAUSE to resume cooking.
5. When cooking is complete, remove drawer from unit. Transfer leg of lamb to a plate. Serve warm.

Spicy Lamb Kebabs

SERVES: 6

PREP TIME: 20 minutes
COOK TIME: 8 minutes

4 eggs, beaten
150 g pistachios, chopped
450 g minced lamb
32 g plain flour
20 g flat-leaf parsley, chopped
2 tsps. chilli flakes
4 garlic cloves, minced
30 ml fresh lemon juice
2 tsps. cumin seeds
1 tsp. fennel seeds
2 tsps. dried mint
2 tsps. salt
Olive oil
1 tsp. coriander seeds
1 tsp. freshly ground black pepper

1. Mix lamb, pistachios, eggs, lemon juice, chilli flakes, flour, cumin seeds, fennel seeds, coriander seeds, mint, parsley, salt and black pepper in a large bowl.
2. Thread the lamb mixture onto metal skewers to form sausages and coat with olive oil.
3. Install a crisper plate in Zone 1 drawer. Place the skewers in the drawer, then insert drawer in unit.
4. Select Zone 1, select ROAST, set temperature to 190°C, and set time to 8 minutes. Press the START/PAUSE button to begin cooking.
5. With 4 minutes remaining, press START/PAUSE to pause the unit. Remove the drawer from unit and flip the skewers over. Reinsert drawer in unit and press START/PAUSE to resume cooking.
6. When cooking is complete, remove drawer from unit. Transfer the skewers to a plate. Serve hot.

Lamb with Potatoes

SERVES: 2

PREP TIME: 20 minutes
COOK TIME: 30 minutes

225 g lamb meat
2 small potatoes, peeled and halved
½ small onion, peeled and halved
1 garlic clove, crushed
½ tbsp. dried rosemary, crushed
5 ml olive oil

1. Rub the lamb evenly with garlic and rosemary.
2. Add potatoes in a large bowl and stir in the olive oil and onions.
3. Insert a crisper plate in both drawers. Place lamb in the Zone 1 drawer, then insert drawer in unit. Place vegetables in the Zone 2 drawer, then insert drawer in unit.
4. Select Zone 1, select ROAST, set temperature to 190°C, and set time to 25 minutes. Select Zone 2, select ROAST, set temperature to 200°C, and set time to 30 minutes. Select SYNC. Press the START/PAUSE button to begin cooking.
5. When the Zone 1 and 2 times reach 15 minutes, press START/PAUSE to pause the unit. Remove the drawers from unit and flip the lamb and vegetables over. Reinsert drawers in unit and press START/PAUSE to resume cooking.
6. When cooking is complete, serve lamb with vegetables.

Italian Lamb Chops with Avocado Mayo

SERVES: 2

PREP TIME: 5 minutes
COOK TIME: 12 minutes

2 lamp chops
2 tsps. Italian herbs
2 avocados
120 ml mayonnaise
15 ml lemon juice

1. Season the lamb chops with the Italian herbs, then set aside for 5 minutes.
2. Install a crisper plate in Zone 1 drawer. Place lamb chops in the drawer, then insert drawer in unit.
3. Select Zone 1, select AIR FRY, set temperature to 200°C, and set time to 12 minutes. Press the START/PAUSE button to begin cooking.
4. With 6 minutes remaining, press START/PAUSE to pause the unit. Remove the drawer from unit and flip the lamb chops over. Reinsert drawer in unit and press START/PAUSE to resume cooking.
5. In the meantime, halve the avocados and open to remove the pits. Spoon the flesh into a blender.
6. Add the mayonnaise and lemon juice and pulse until a smooth consistency is achieved.
7. When cooking is complete, remove drawer from unit. Transfer lamb chops to a plate. Serve warm with the avocado mayo.

Spiced Lamb Steaks

SERVES: 3

PREP TIME: 15 minutes
COOK TIME: 15 minutes

½ onion, roughly chopped
680 g boneless lamb sirloin steaks
5 garlic cloves, peeled
6 g fresh ginger, peeled
1 tsp. garam masala
1 tsp. ground fennel
½ tsp. ground cumin
½ tsp. ground cinnamon
½ tsp. cayenne pepper
Salt and black pepper, to taste

1. Put the onion, garlic, ginger, and spices in a blender and pulse until smooth.
2. Coat the lamb steaks with this mixture on both sides and refrigerate to marinate for about 24 hours.
3. Install a crisper plate in Zone 1 drawer. Place lamb steaks in the drawer, then insert drawer in unit.
4. Select Zone 1, select ROAST, set temperature to 200°C, and set time to 15 minutes. Press the START/PAUSE button to begin cooking.
5. With 8 minutes remaining, press START/PAUSE to pause the unit. Remove the drawer from unit and flip the lamb steaks over. Reinsert drawer in unit and press START/PAUSE to resume cooking.
6. When cooking is complete, remove drawer from unit. Transfer lamb steaks to a plate. Serve warm.

Roasted Lamb

SERVES: 4

PREP TIME: 15 minutes
COOK TIME: 1 hour

1.1 kg half lamb leg roast, slits carved
2 garlic cloves, sliced into smaller slithers
1 tbsp. dried rosemary
15 ml olive oil
Cracked Himalayan rock salt and cracked peppercorns, to taste

1. Insert the garlic slithers in the slits and brush with rosemary, oil, salt, and black pepper.
2. Install a crisper plate in Zone 1 drawer. Place the lamb in the drawer, then insert drawer in unit.
3. Select Zone 1, select ROAST, set temperature to 200°C, and set time to 1 hour. Press the START/PAUSE button to begin cooking.
4. With 30 minutes remaining, press START/PAUSE to pause the unit. Remove the drawer from unit and flip the lamb over. Reinsert drawer in unit and press START/PAUSE to resume cooking.
5. When cooking is complete, remove drawer from unit. Transfer the lamb to a plate. Serve warm.

Greek Lamb Pitta Pockets

SERVES: 4

PREP TIME: 15 minutes
COOK TIME: 10 minutes

For the Dressing:
240 ml plain yoghurt
15 ml lemon juice
1 tsp. dried dill, crushed
1 tsp. ground oregano
½ tsp. salt
For the Meatballs:
225 g minced lamb
10 g diced onion
1 tsp. dried parsley
1 tsp. dried dill, crushed
¼ tsp. oregano
¼ tsp. coriander
¼ tsp. ground cumin
¼ tsp. salt
4 pitta halves
Suggested Toppings:
1 red onion, slivered
1 medium cucumber, deseeded, thinly sliced
Crumbled Feta cheese
Sliced black olives
Chopped fresh peppers

1. Stir the dressing ingredients together in a small bowl and refrigerate while preparing lamb.
2. Combine all meatball ingredients in a large bowl and stir to distribute seasonings.
3. Shape meat mixture into 12 small meatballs, rounded or slightly flattened if you prefer.
4. Insert a crisper plate in both drawers. Place half of the meatballs in a single layer in each drawer.
5. Select Zone 1, select AIR FRY, set temperature to 200°C, and set time to 10 minutes. Select MATCH COOK to match Zone 2 settings to Zone 1. Select START/PAUSE to begin cooking.
6. When the Zone 1 and 2 times reach 5 minutes, press START/PAUSE to pause the unit. Remove the drawers from unit and flip the meatballs over. Reinsert drawers in unit and press START/PAUSE to resume cooking.
7. When cooking is complete, transfer meatballs and drain on paper towels.
8. To serve, pile meatballs and the choice of toppings in pitta pockets and drizzle with dressing.

CHAPTER 8

BEEF

Tasty Beef Stuffed Bell Peppers ········ 57
Beef Sausages ········ 57
Beef Braising Steak with Brussels Sprouts ········ 58
Simple Beef Burgers ········ 58
Italian Beef Meatballs ········ 59
Mushroom and Beef Meatloaf ········ 59
Beef Jerky ········ 60
Buttered Rib Eye Steak ········ 60
Air Fried Beef Ribs ········ 61
Easy Rib Steak ········ 61
Veal Rolls ········ 62
Crispy Sirloin Steak ········ 62

Tasty Beef Stuffed Bell Peppers

SERVES: 4

PREP TIME: 20 minutes
COOK TIME: 30 minutes

½ medium onion, chopped
450 g lean beef, minced
80 g jasmine rice, cooked
80 g light Mexican cheese, shredded and divided
4 bell peppers, tops and seeds removed
5 ml olive oil
2 garlic cloves, minced
1 tsp. dried basil, crushed
1 tsp. garlic salt
½ tsp. red chilli powder
Ground black pepper, as required
225 g tomato sauce, divided
10 ml Worcestershire sauce

1. Heat olive oil in a medium frying pan over medium heat and add onion and garlic.
2. Sauté for about 5 minutes and add the minced beef, basil, and spices.
3. Cook for about 10 minutes and drain off the excess grease from frying pan.
4. Stir in the rice, half of the cheese, ⅔ of the tomato sauce and Worcestershire sauce and mix well.
5. Stuff the beef mixture in each bell pepper.
6. Install a crisper plate in Zone 1 drawer. Place the bell peppers in the drawer, then insert drawer in unit.
7. Select Zone 1, select AIR FRY, set temperature to 200°C, and set time to 15 minutes. Press the START/PAUSE button to begin cooking.
8. With 10 minutes remaining, press START/PAUSE to pause the unit. Remove the drawer from unit and top with the remaining tomato sauce and cheese. Reinsert drawer in unit and press START/PAUSE to resume cooking.
9. When cooking is complete, remove drawer from unit. Transfer bell peppers to a plate. Serve warm.

Beef Sausages

SERVES: 4

PREP TIME: 5 minutes
COOK TIME: 15 minutes

4 (85 g) beef sausages

1. Install a crisper plate in Zone 1 drawer. Place the beef sausages in the drawer, then insert drawer in unit.
2. Select Zone 1, select AIR FRY, set temperature to 190°C, and set time to 15 minutes. Press the START/PAUSE button to begin cooking.
3. With 8 minutes remaining, press START/PAUSE to pause the unit. Remove the drawer from unit and flip the beef sausages over. Reinsert drawer in unit and press START/PAUSE to resume cooking.
4. When cooking is complete, remove drawer from unit. Transfer the beef sausages to a plate. Serve hot.

Beef Braising Steak with Brussels Sprouts

SERVES: 4

PREP TIME: 20 minutes
COOK TIME: 25 minutes

450 g beef braising steak
30 ml vegetable oil
15 ml red wine vinegar
1 tsp. fine sea salt
½ tsp. ground black pepper
1 tsp. smoked paprika
1 tsp. onion powder
½ tsp. garlic powder
225 g Brussels sprouts, cleaned and halved
½ tsp. fennel seeds
1 tsp. dried basil
1 tsp. dried sage

1. Massage the beef with the vegetable oil, wine vinegar, salt, black pepper, paprika, onion powder, and garlic powder, coating it well.
2. Allow to marinate for a minimum of 3 hours.
3. Insert a crisper plate in both drawers. Remove the beef from the marinade and put in the Zone 1 drawer, then insert drawer in unit. Place Brussels sprouts in the Zone 2 drawer along with the fennel seeds, basil, and sage, then insert drawer in unit.
4. Select Zone 1, select ROAST, set temperature to 200°C, and set time to 20 minutes. Select Zone 2, select AIR FRY, set temperature to 200°C, and set time to 25 minutes. Select SYNC. Press the START/PAUSE button to begin cooking.
5. When the Zone 1 and Zone 2 times reach 10 minutes, press START/PAUSE and remove drawers from unit. In Zone 1, flip the beef over. In Zone 2, shake for 10 seconds. Reinsert drawers in unit and press START/PAUSE to resume cooking.
6. When cooking is complete, serve beef with Brussels sprouts.

Simple Beef Burgers

SERVES: 6

PREP TIME: 20 minutes
COOK TIME: 16 minutes

900 g minced beef
12 cheddar cheese slices
12 burger buns
90 ml tomato ketchup
Salt and black pepper, to taste

1. Mix the beef, salt and black pepper in a bowl.
2. Make small equal-sized patties from the beef mixture.
3. Insert a crisper plate in both drawers. Place half of patties in a single layer in each drawer.
4. Select Zone 1, select BAKE, set temperature to 200°C, and set time to 16 minutes. Select MATCH COOK to match Zone 2 settings to Zone 1. Select START/PAUSE to begin cooking.
5. When the Zone 1 and 2 times reach 8 minutes, press START/PAUSE to pause the unit. Remove the drawers from unit and flip the patties over. Reinsert drawers in unit and press START/PAUSE to resume cooking.
6. When cooking is complete, transfer pork chops to a plate. top each patty with 1 cheese slice. Arrange the patties between rolls and drizzle with ketchup. Serve hot.

Italian Beef Meatballs

SERVES: 6

PREP TIME: 10 minutes
COOK TIME: 16 minutes

2 large eggs
900 g minced beef
15 g fresh parsley, chopped
150 g panko breadcrumbs
30 g Parmesan cheese, grated
1 tsp. dried oregano
1 small garlic clove, chopped
Salt and black pepper, to taste
5 ml vegetable oil

1. Mix beef with all other ingredients in a bowl until well combined. Make equal-sized balls from the mixture.
2. Insert a crisper plate in both drawers. Place half of meatballs in a single layer in each drawer.
3. Select Zone 1, select AIR FRY, set temperature to 180°C, and set time to 16 minutes. Select MATCH COOK to match Zone 2 settings to Zone 1. Select START/PAUSE to begin cooking.
4. When the Zone 1 and 2 times reach 8 minutes, press START/PAUSE to pause the unit. Remove the drawers from unit and flip the meatballs over. Reinsert drawers in unit and press START/PAUSE to resume cooking.
5. When cooking is complete, transfer meatballs to a plate. Serve warm.

Mushroom and Beef Meatloaf

SERVES: 4

PREP TIME: 10 minutes
COOK TIME: 25 minutes

450 g minced beef
1 egg, beaten
1 mushrooms, sliced
1 tbsp. thyme
1 small onion, chopped
15 g bread crumbs
Ground black pepper, to taste

1. Put all the ingredients into a large bowl and combine entirely.
2. Transfer the meatloaf mixture into the loaf pan.
3. Install a crisper plate in Zone 1 drawer. Place loaf pan in the drawer, then insert drawer in unit.
4. Select Zone 1, select BAKE, set temperature to 200°C, and set time to 25 minutes. Press the START/PAUSE button to begin cooking.
5. When cooking is complete, remove the meatloaf from unit. Slice up before serving.

Beef Jerky

SERVES: 3

PREP TIME: 20 minutes
COOK TIME: 5 hours

450 g beef silverside, cut into thin strips
100 g dark brown sugar
120 ml soy sauce
60 ml Worcestershire sauce
15 ml chilli pepper sauce
1 tbsp. hickory liquid smoke
1 tsp. garlic powder
1 tsp. onion powder
1 tsp. cayenne pepper
½ tsp. smoked paprika
½ tsp. ground black pepper

1. Mix the brown sugar, all sauces, liquid smoke, and spices in a bowl.
2. Coat the beef strips with this marinade generously and marinate overnight.
3. Place a single layer of beef strips in the drawer. Then install the crisper plate in the drawer on top of the beef strips and place another layer of beef strips on the crisper plate.
4. Select Zone 1, select DEHYDRATE, set temperature to 70°C, and set time to 5 hours. Press the START/PAUSE button to begin cooking.
5. When cooking is complete, remove drawer from unit. Transfer beef jerky to a plate. Serve warm.

Buttered Rib Eye Steak

SERVES: 2

PREP TIME: 20 minutes
COOK TIME: 18 minutes

110 g unsalted butter, softened
8 g fresh parsley, chopped
2 (225 g) rib eye steaks
2 tsps. garlic, minced
5 ml Worcestershire sauce
15 ml olive oil
Salt and black pepper, to taste

1. Mix the butter, parsley, garlic, Worcestershire sauce, and salt in a bowl.
2. Place the butter mixture onto a parchment paper, roll into a log and refrigerate for about 3 hours.
3. Rub the steak generously with olive oil, salt and black pepper.
4. Install a crisper plate in Zone 1 drawer. Place the steaks in the drawer, then insert drawer in unit.
5. Select Zone 1, select AIR FRY, set temperature to 200°C, and set time to 18 minutes. Press the START/PAUSE button to begin cooking.
6. With 8 minutes remaining, press START/PAUSE to pause the unit. Remove the drawer from unit and flip the steaks over. Reinsert drawer in unit and press START/PAUSE to resume cooking.
7. When cooking is complete, remove drawer from unit. Transfer the steaks to a plate and cut into desired size slices. Cut the butter log into slices and top over the steak to serve.

Air Fried Beef Ribs

SERVES: 4

PREP TIME: 20 minutes
COOK TIME: 16 minutes

450 g meaty beef ribs, rinsed and drained
45 ml apple cider vinegar
50 g coriander, finely chopped
4 g fresh basil leaves, chopped
2 garlic cloves, finely chopped
1 chipotle powder
1 tsp. fennel seeds
1 tsp. hot paprika
coarse salt and black pepper, to taste
120 ml vegetable oil

1. Coat the ribs with the remaining ingredients and refrigerate for at least 3 hours.
2. Install a crisper plate in Zone 1 drawer. Separate the ribs from the marinade and put in the drawer, then insert drawer in unit.
3. Select Zone 1, select AIR FRY, set temperature to 180°C, and set time to 16 minutes. Press the START/PAUSE button to begin cooking.
4. With 8 minutes remaining, press START/PAUSE to pause the unit. Remove the drawer from unit and flip the ribs over. Reinsert drawer in unit and press START/PAUSE to resume cooking.
5. When cooking is complete, remove drawer from unit. Transfer the ribs to a plate. Pour the remaining marinade over the ribs before serving.

Easy Rib Steak

SERVES: 4

PREP TIME: 10 minutes
COOK TIME: 20 minutes

900 g rib steak
400 g steak rub
15 ml olive oil

1. Rub the steak generously with steak rub, salt and black pepper, and coat with olive oil.
2. Install a crisper plate in Zone 1 drawer. Place the steak in the drawer, then insert drawer in unit.
3. Select Zone 1, select ROAST, set temperature to 200°C, and set time to 20 minutes. Press the START/PAUSE button to begin cooking.
4. With 10 minutes remaining, press START/PAUSE to pause the unit. Remove the drawer from unit and flip the steak over. Reinsert drawer in unit and press START/PAUSE to resume cooking.
5. When cooking is complete, remove drawer from unit. Transfer the steak to a plate and cut into desired size slices to serve.

(Note: To prepare the Steak Rub - 2 tbsps. fresh cracked black pepper, 2 tbsps. coarse salt, 2 tbsps. paprika, 1 tbsp. crushed red pepper flakes, 1 tbsp. crushed coriander seeds (not ground), 1 tbsp. garlic powder, 1 tbsp. onion powder, 2 tsps. cayenne pepper. Mix all ingredients in a medium bowl and stir well to combine.)

Veal Rolls

SERVES: 4

PREP TIME: 15 minutes
COOK TIME: 15 minutes

4 (170 g) veal cutlets
6 g fresh sage leaves
4 cured ham slices
15 g unsalted butter, melted
Salt and black pepper, to taste

1. Season the veal cutlets with salt and roll them up tightly.
2. Wrap 1 ham slice around each roll and coat with 1 tbsp. of the butter. Top rolls with the sage leaves.
3. Install a crisper plate in Zone 1 drawer. Place rolls in the drawer, then insert drawer in unit.
4. Select Zone 1, select AIR FRY, set temperature to 200°C, and set time to 15 minutes. Press the START/PAUSE button to begin cooking.
5. With 7 minutes remaining, press START/PAUSE to pause the unit. Remove the drawer from unit and flip the rolls over. Reinsert drawer in unit and press START/PAUSE to resume cooking.
6. When cooking is complete, remove drawer from unit. Transfer rolls to a plate. Serve warm.

Crispy Sirloin Steak

SERVES: 2

PREP TIME: 15 minutes
COOK TIME: 18 minutes

120 g white flour
2 eggs
100 g panko breadcrumbs
2 (170 g) sirloin steaks, pounded
1 tsp. garlic powder
1 tsp. onion powder
Salt and black pepper, to taste

1. Place the flour in a shallow bowl and whisk eggs in a second dish.
2. Mix the panko breadcrumbs and spices in a third bowl.
3. Rub the steaks with flour, dip into the eggs and coat with breadcrumb mixture.
4. Install a crisper plate in Zone 1 drawer. Place steaks in the drawer, then insert drawer in unit.
5. Select Zone 1, select AIR FRY, set temperature to 200°C, and set time to 18 minutes. Press the START/PAUSE button to begin cooking.
6. With 8 minutes remaining, press START/PAUSE to pause the unit. Remove the drawer from unit and flip the steaks over. Reinsert drawer in unit and press START/PAUSE to resume cooking.
7. When cooking is complete, remove drawer from unit. Transfer steaks to a plate and cut into desired size slices to serve.

CHAPTER 9
SNACK AND DESSERT

Crispy Spiced Chickpeas ········ 64

Apple Crisps ········ 64

Cajun Courgette Crisps ········ 65

Air Fried Olives ········ 65

Sunflower Seeds Bread ········ 66

Flavour-Packed Clafoutis ········ 66

Chocolate Coconut Brownies ········ 67

Classic Buttermilk Scones ········ 67

Cheesy Bread Rolls ········ 68

Decadent Cheesecake ········ 68

Spiced Mixed Nuts ········ 69

Buffalo Cauliflower with Sour Dip ········ 69

Baked Halloumi with Greek Salsa ········ 70

Stuffed Apples ········ 70

Crispy Spiced Chickpeas

SERVES: 4

PREP TIME: 5 minutes
COOK TIME: 10 minutes

1 tin (425 g) chickpeas, rinsed and dried with paper towels
15 ml olive oil
½ tsp. dried rosemary
½ tsp. dried parsley
½ tsp. dried chives
¼ tsp. mustard powder
¼ tsp. sweet paprika
¼ tsp. cayenne pepper
Coarse salt and freshly ground black pepper, to taste

1. In a large bowl, combine all the ingredients, except for the coarse salt and black pepper, and toss until the chickpeas are evenly coated in the herbs and spices.
2. Install a crisper plate in Zone 1 drawer. Scrape the chickpeas and seasonings into the drawer, then insert drawer in unit.
3. Select Zone 1, select AIR FRY, set temperature to 180°C, and set time to 10 minutes. Press the START/PAUSE button to begin cooking.
4. With 5 minutes remaining, press START/PAUSE to pause the unit. Remove the drawer from unit and shake for 10 seconds. Reinsert drawer in unit and press START/PAUSE to resume cooking.
5. When cooking is complete, remove drawer from unit. Transfer crispy chickpeas to a bowl. Sprinkle with coarse salt and black pepper and serve warm.

Apple Crisps

SERVES: 1

PREP TIME: 5 minutes
COOK TIME: 30 minutes

1 Pink Lady apple

1. Core the apple with an apple corer, leaving apple whole. Cut the apple into 3-mm-thick slices.
2. Install a crisper plate in Zone 1 drawer. Place apple slices in the drawer, staggering slices as much as possible, then insert drawer in unit.
3. Select Zone 1, select AIR FRY, set temperature to 150°C, and set time to 30 minutes. Press the START/PAUSE button to begin cooking, until the slices are dry and some are lightly browned, turning 4 times with tongs to separate and rotate them from top to bottom.
4. When cooking is complete, remove drawer from unit. Place the slices in a single layer on a wire rack to cool. Apples will become crisper as they cool. Serve immediately.

Cajun Courgette Crisps

SERVES: 4

PREP TIME: 5 minutes
COOK TIME: 15 to 16 minutes

2 large courgettes, cut into 3-mm-thick slices
2 tsps. Cajun seasoning
Cooking spray

1. Put the courgette slices in a medium bowl and spray them generously with cooking spray.
2. Sprinkle the Cajun seasoning over the courgette and stir to make sure they are evenly coated with oil and seasoning.
3. Insert a crisper plate in both drawer and spray lightly with cooking spray. Place half of the slices in a single layer in each drawer.
4. Select Zone 1, select AIR FRY, set temperature to 200°C, and set time to 25 minutes. Select MATCH COOK to match Zone 2 settings to Zone 1. Select START/PAUSE to begin cooking.
5. When the Zone 1 and 2 times reach 12 minutes, press START/PAUSE to pause the unit. Remove the drawers from unit and flip the courgette slices over. Reinsert drawers in unit and press START/PAUSE to resume cooking.
6. When cooking is complete, transfer courgette slices to a plate. Serve warm.

Air Fried Olives

SERVES: 4

PREP TIME: 5 minutes
COOK TIME: 8 minutes

1 (160 g) jar pitted green olives
50 g plain flour
Salt and pepper, to taste
50 g bread crumbs
1 egg
Cooking spray

1. Remove the olives from the jar and dry thoroughly with paper towels.
2. In a small bowl, combine the flour with salt and pepper to taste. Place the bread crumbs in another small bowl. In a third small bowl, beat the egg.
3. Dip the olives in the flour, then the egg, and then the bread crumbs.
4. Install a crisper plate in Zone 1 drawer and spritz with cooking spray. Place breaded olives in the drawer, then insert drawer in unit.
5. Select Zone 1, select AIR FRY, set temperature to 200°C, and set time to 8 minutes. Press the START/PAUSE button to begin cooking.
6. With 4 minutes remaining, press START/PAUSE to pause the unit. Remove the drawer from unit and flip the breaded olives over. Reinsert drawer in unit and press START/PAUSE to resume cooking.
7. When cooking is complete, remove drawer from unit. Transfer breaded olives to a plate. Cool before serving.

Sunflower Seeds Bread

SERVES: 4

PREP TIME: 15 minutes
COOK TIME: 18 minutes

85 g whole wheat flour
85 g plain flour
45 g sunflower seeds
240 ml lukewarm water
½ sachet instant yeast
1 tsp. salt

1. Grease a 18 x 10 cm cake pan.
2. Mix together flours, sunflower seeds, yeast and salt in a bowl.
3. Add water slowly and knead for about 5 minutes until a dough is formed.
4. Cover the dough with a clingfilm and keep in warm place for about half an hour.
5. Arrange the dough into the cake pan.
6. Install a crisper plate in Zone 1 drawer. Place the cake pan in the drawer, then insert drawer in unit.
7. Select Zone 1, select BAKE, set temperature to 200°C, and set time to 18 minutes. Press the START/PAUSE button to begin cooking.
8. When cooking is complete, remove drawer from unit. Serve warm.

Flavour-Packed Clafoutis

SERVES: 4

PREP TIME: 10 minutes
COOK TIME: 25 minutes

220 g fresh cherries, pitted
30 g flour
1 egg
15 g butter
45 ml vodka
30 g sugar
Pinch of salt
120 ml sour cream
30 g icing sugar

1. Grease a 18x13 cm baking pan lightly.
2. Mix cherries and vodka in a bowl.
3. Sift together flour, sugar and salt in another bowl.
4. Stir in the sour cream and egg until a smooth dough is formed.
5. Transfer the dough evenly into the baking pan and top with the cherry mixture and butter.
6. Install a crisper plate in Zone 1 drawer. Place the baking pan in the drawer, then insert drawer in unit.
7. Select Zone 1, select BAKE, set temperature to 180°C, and set time to 25 minutes. Press the START/PAUSE button to begin cooking.
8. When cooking is complete, dust with icing sugar and serve warm.

Chocolate Coconut Brownies

SERVES: 6

PREP TIME: 15 minutes
COOK TIME: 15 minutes

120 ml coconut oil
60 g dark chocolate
200 g sugar
37 ml water
4 whisked eggs
¼ tsp. ground cinnamon
½ tsp. ground star anise
¼ tsp. coconut extract
½ tsp. vanilla extract
15 ml honey
60 g flour
60 g desiccated coconut
Sugar, for dusting

1. Melt the coconut oil and dark chocolate in the microwave.
2. Combine with the sugar, water, eggs, cinnamon, anise, coconut extract, vanilla, and honey in a large bowl.
3. Stir in the flour and desiccated coconut. Incorporate everything well.
4. Lightly grease a 18x13 cm baking dish with butter. Transfer the mixture to the dish.
5. Install a crisper plate in Zone 1 drawer. Place the baking dish in the drawer, then insert drawer in unit.
6. Select Zone 1, select BAKE, set temperature to 180°C, and set time to 15 minutes. Press the START/PAUSE button to begin cooking.
7. When cooking is complete, remove drawer from unit and allow to cool slightly.
8. Take care when taking it out of the baking dish. Slice it into squares.
9. Dust with sugar before serving.

Classic Buttermilk Scones

SERVES: 4

PREP TIME: 15 minutes
COOK TIME: 8 minutes

60 g all purpose flour
150 g plain flour
4 g baking soda
3 g baking powder
75 g unsalted butter, cut into cubes
180 ml buttermilk
4 g granulated sugar
Salt, to taste

1. Grease a 13-cm pie dish lightly.
2. Sift together flours, baking soda, baking powder, sugar and salt in a large bowl.
3. Add cold butter and mix until a coarse crumb is formed.
4. Stir in the buttermilk slowly and mix until a dough is formed.
5. Press the dough into 1-cm thickness onto a floured surface and cut out circles with a 4-cm round cookie cutter.
6. Arrange the scones in the pie dish in a single layer and brush butter on them.
7. Install a crisper plate in Zone 1 drawer. Place the pie dish in the drawer, then insert drawer in unit.
8. Select Zone 1, select BAKE, set temperature to 200°C, and set time to 8 minutes. Press the START/PAUSE button to begin cooking, until golden brown.
9. When cooking is complete, serve warm.

Cheesy Bread Rolls

SERVES: 2

PREP TIME: 10 minutes
COOK TIME: 6 minutes

Cooking spray
2 bread rolls
60 g Parmesan cheese, grated
30 g unsalted butter, melted
½ tsp. garlic bread seasoning mix

1. Cut the bread rolls in slits and stuff cheese in the slits.
2. Top with butter and garlic bread seasoning mix.
3. Install a crisper plate in Zone 1 drawer and spray with cooking spray. Place dinner rolls in the drawer, then insert drawer in unit.
4. Select Zone 1, select BAKE, set temperature to 180°C, and set time to 6 minutes. Press the START/PAUSE button to begin cooking.
5. With 3 minutes remaining, press START/PAUSE to pause the unit. Remove the drawer from unit and flip the dinner rolls over. Reinsert drawer in unit and press START/PAUSE to resume cooking.
6. When cooking is complete, remove drawer from unit. Transfer bread rolls to a plate. Serve warm.

Decadent Cheesecake

SERVES: 6

PREP TIME: 15 minutes
COOK TIME: 33 minutes

3 eggs, separated
170 g white chocolate, chopped
120 g cream cheese, softened
14 g cocoa powder
60 g apricot jam
16 g icing sugar

1. Grease a 18 x 10 cm cake pan lightly.
2. Refrigerate egg whites in a bowl to chill before using.
3. Microwave chocolate and cream cheese on high for about 3 minutes.
4. Remove from microwave and whisk in the egg yolks.
5. Whisk together egg whites until firm peaks form and combine with the chocolate mixture. Transfer the mixture into the cake pan.
6. Install a crisper plate in Zone 1 drawer. Place the cake pan in the drawer, then insert drawer in unit.
7. Select Zone 1, select BAKE, set temperature to 140°C, and set time to 30 minutes. Press the START/PAUSE button to begin cooking.
8. When cooking is complete, remove drawer from unit. Dust with icing sugar and spread jam on top to serve.

Spiced Mixed Nuts

SERVES: 4

PREP TIME: 5 minutes
COOK TIME: 6 minutes

75 g raw cashews
55 g raw pecan halves
50 g raw walnut halves
70 g raw whole almonds
30 ml olive oil
12 g light brown sugar
1 tsp. chopped fresh rosemary leaves
1 tsp. chopped fresh thyme leaves
1 tsp. coarse salt
½ tsp. ground coriander
¼ tsp. onion powder
¼ tsp. freshly ground black pepper
⅛ tsp. garlic powder

1. In a large bowl, combine all the ingredients and toss until the nuts are evenly coated in the herbs, spices, and sugar.
2. Install a crisper plate in Zone 1 drawer. Scrape the nuts and seasonings into the drawer, then insert drawer in unit.
3. Select Zone 1, select AIR FRY, set temperature to 180°C, and set time to 6 minutes. Press the START/PAUSE button to begin cooking.
4. With 3 minutes remaining, press START/PAUSE to pause the unit. Remove the drawer from unit and shake for 10 seconds. Reinsert drawer in unit and press START/PAUSE to resume cooking, until golden brown and fragrant.
5. When cooking is complete, remove drawer from unit. Transfer the cocktail nuts to a bowl and serve warm.

Buffalo Cauliflower with Sour Dip

SERVES: 6

PREP TIME: 10 minutes
COOK TIME: 20 minutes

1 large head cauliflower, separated into small florets
15 ml olive oil
½ tsp. garlic powder
80 ml low-sodium hot wing sauce, divided
160 ml nonfat Greek yoghurt
½ tsp. Tabasco sauce
1 celery stalk, chopped
10 g crumbled blue stilton cheese

1. In a large bowl, toss the cauliflower florets with the olive oil. Sprinkle with the garlic powder and toss again to coat.
2. Insert a crisper plate in both drawers. Place half of the cauliflower in each drawer.
3. Select Zone 1, select AIR FRY, set temperature to 200°C, and set time to 20 minutes. Select MATCH COOK to match Zone 2 settings to Zone 1. Select START/PAUSE to begin cooking.
4. When the Zone 1 and 2 times reach 10 minutes, press START/PAUSE to pause the unit. Remove the drawers from unit and shake for 10 seconds. Reinsert drawers in unit and press START/PAUSE to resume cooking.
5. When cooking is complete, transfer the cauliflower to a serving bowl and and toss with the wing sauce.
6. In a small bowl, stir together the yoghurt, Tabasco sauce, celery, and blue stilton cheese. Serve the cauliflower with the dip.

Baked Halloumi with Greek Salsa

SERVES: 4

PREP TIME: 15 minutes
COOK TIME: 6 minutes

For the Salsa:
1 small shallot, finely diced
3 garlic cloves, minced
30 ml fresh lemon juice
30 ml extra-virgin olive oil
1 tsp. freshly cracked black pepper
Pinch of coarse salt
75 g finely diced English cucumber
1 plum tomato, deseeded and finely diced
2 tsps. chopped fresh parsley
1 tsp. snipped fresh dill
1 tsp. snipped fresh oregano
For the Cheese:
225 g Halloumi cheese, sliced into 1-cm-thick pieces
15 ml extra-virgin olive oil

1. For the salsa: Combine the shallot, garlic, lemon juice, olive oil, pepper, and salt in a medium bowl. Add the cucumber, tomato, parsley, dill, and oregano. Toss gently to combine; set aside.
2. For the cheese: Place the cheese slices in a medium bowl. Drizzle with the olive oil. Toss gently to coat.
3. Install a crisper plate in Zone 1 drawer. Place the cheese in the drawer, then insert drawer in unit.
4. Select Zone 1, select BAKE, set temperature to 190°C, and set time to 6 minutes. Press the START/PAUSE button to begin cooking.
5. When cooking is complete, remove drawer from unit. Divide the cheese among four serving plates. Top with the salsa and serve immediately.

Stuffed Apples

SERVES: 4

PREP TIME: 10 minutes
COOK TIME: 13 minutes

4 small firm apples, cored
80 g golden sultanas
65 g blanched almonds
60 g sugar, divided
120 ml whipped cream
½ tsp. vanilla extract

1. Grease a 18x13 cm baking dish lightly.
2. Put sultanas, almond and half of sugar in a food processor and pulse until chopped.
3. Stuff the sultana mixture inside each apple and arrange the apples in the prepared baking dish.
4. Install a crisper plate in Zone 1 drawer. Place the baking dish in the drawer, then insert drawer in unit.
5. Select Zone 1, select BAKE, set temperature to 180°C, and set time to 10 minutes. Press the START/PAUSE button to begin cooking.
6. When cooking is complete, remove drawer from unit.
7. Put cream, remaining sugar and vanilla extract on medium heat in a pan and cook for about 3 minutes, continuously stirring.
8. Remove from the heat and serve apple with vanilla sauce.

APPENDIX 1:
NINJA DUAL ZONE AIR FRY TIMETABLE

Air Fry Cooking Chart

INGREDIENT	AMOUNT	PREPARATION	TOSS IN OIL	TEMP	COOK TIME
VEGETABLES					
Asparagus	200g	Whole, stems trimmed	2 tsp	200°C	8-12 mins
Beetroot	6 small or 4 large (about 1kg)	Whole	None	200°C	35-45 mins
Bell peppers (for roasting)	2 peppers	Whole	None	200°C	16 mins
Broccoli	1 head (400g)	Cut in 2.5cm florets	1 Tbsp	200°C	9 mins
Brussel sprouts	500g	Cut in half, stem removed	1 Tbsp	200°C	15-20 mins
Butternut squash	500g-750g	Cut in 2.5cm pieces	1 Tbsp	200°C	20-25 mins
Carrots	500g	Peeled, cut in 1.5cm pieces	1 Tbsp	200°C	13-16 mins
Cauliflower	1 head (900g)	Cut in 2.5cm florets	2 Tbsp	200°C	15-20 mins
Corn on the cob	4 ears	Whole ears, husks removed	1 Tbsp	200°C	12-15 mins
Courgette	500g	Cut in quarters lengthwise, then cut in 2.5cm pieces	1 Tbsp	200°C	15-18 mins
Fine green beans	200g	Trimmed	1 Tbsp	200°C	8 mins
Kale (for crisps)	100g	Torn in pieces, stems removed	None	150°C	8 mins
Mushrooms	225g	Wiped, cut in quarters	1 Tbsp	200°C	7 mins
Potatoes, white e.g. King Edward, Maris Piper or Russet	750g	Cut in 2.5cm wedges	1 Tbsp	200°C	18-20 mins
	450g	Hand-cut chips, thin	½-3 Tbsp, vegetable oil	200°C	20-24 mins
	450g	Hand-cut chips, thick	½-3 Tbsp, vegetable oil	200°C	23-26 mins
	4 whole (200g each)	Pierced with fork 3 times	None	200°C	25 mins
Potatoes, sweet	750g	Cut in 2.5cm chunks	1 Tbsp	200°C	15-20 mins
	4 whole (225g each)	Pierced with fork 3 times	None	200°C	30-35 mins
POULTRY					
Chicken breasts	2 breasts (200g each)	None	Brushed with oil	190°C	22-25 mins
	4 breasts (150-175g each)	None	Brushed with oil	190°C	34 mins
Chicken thighs	4 thighs (200g each)	Bone in	Brushed with oil	200°C	22-28 mins
	4 thighs (100g each)	Boneless	Brushed with oil	200°C	18-22 mins
Chicken wings	1kg	Drumettes & flats	1 Tbsp	200°C	33 mins
FISH & SEAFOOD					
Fish cakes	2 cakes (145g each)	None	Brushed with oil	200°C	15 mins
Salmon fillets	2 fillets	None	Brushed with oil	200°C	10-13 mins
Prawns	16 large	Whole, peeled, tails on	1 Tbsp	200°C	7-10 mins

Air Fry Cooking Chart

INGREDIENT	AMOUNT	PREPARATION	TOSS IN OIL	TEMP	COOK TIME
BEEF					
Burgers	4 quarter-pounders	2.5cm thick	None	190°C	12 mins
Steaks	2 steaks (230g each)	Whole	None	200°C	22 mins
PORK					
Bacon	4 strips, cut in half	None	None	180°C	9 mins
Pork chops	2 thick-cut, bone-in chops	Bone in	Brushed with oil	190°C	19 mins
	4 boneless chops	Boneless	Brushed with oil	190°C	18 mins
Pork loin steaks	2 steaks (400g)	Whole	Brushed with oil	180°C	17 mins
Sausages	4 sausages	Whole	None	200°C	16 mins
Gammon steaks	1 steak (225g)	Cut rind at 2cm, turn over after 5 mins	Brushed with oil	180°C	10 mins
LAMB					
Lamb chops	4 chops (340g)	None	Brushed with oil	200°C	12 mins
Lamb steaks	3 steaks (300g)	None	Brushed with oil	200°C	12 mins
FROZEN FOODS					
Chicken nuggets	1 box (397g)	None	None	200°C	16 mins
Breaded fish fillets	4 fillets (Total 500g)	None	None	200°C	14-16 mins
Fish fingers	10	None	None	200°C	15 mins
French fries	500g	None	None	180°C	20 mins
French fries	1kg	None	None	180°C	42 mins
Sweet potato chips	450g	None	None	190°C	20 mins
Hash browns	7	Single layer	None	200°C	15 mins
Fish fillets in batter	4	Turn halfway	None	180°C	18 mins
Scampi in breadcrumbs	280g	None	None	180°C	12 mins
Prawn tempura	8 prawns (total 140g)	Turn halfway	None	190°C	8-9 mins
Chunky oven chips	500g	None	None	180°C	20 mins
Potato wedges	500g	None	None	180°C	20 mins
Roast potatoes	700g	None	None	190°C	20 mins
Vegan burgers	4	Single layer	None	180°C	10 mins
Battered onion rings	300g	None	None	190°C	14 mins
Breaded garlic mushrooms	300g	None	None	190°C	10-12 mins
Chicken goujons	11	None	None	190°C	8 mins
Chicken Kiev	4	None	None	180°C	15 mins
Yorkshire pudding	8 (total 150g)	None	None	180°C	3-4 mins

Max Crisp Cooking Chart

INGREDIENT	AMOUNT	PREPARATION	TEMP	DEHYDRATE TIME
FROZEN FOOD				
Chicken nuggets	350g (24 nuggets)	None	None	10 mins
Chicken wings	1kg	None	1 Tbsp	17 mins
Popcorn chicken	850g	None	None	6-8 mins
Sweet potato fries	500g	None	1 Tbsp	17 mins
French fries	500g	None	None	8 mins
French fries	1kg	None	None	25 mins
Onion rings	300g	None	None	9 mins

Dehydrate Chart

INGREDIENTS	PREPARATION	TEMP	DEHYDRATE TIME
FRUITS & VEGETABLES			
Apples	Core removed, cut in 3mm slices, rinsed in lemon water, patted dry	60°C	7-8 hours
Asparagus	Cut in 2.5cm pieces, blanched	60°C	6-8 hours
Bananas	Peeled, cut in 3mm slices	60°C	8-10 hours
Beetroot	Peeled, cut in 3mm slices	60°C	6-8 hours
Aubergine	Peeled, cut in 3mm slices, blanched	60°C	6-8 hours
Fresh herbs	Rinsed, patted dry, stems removed	60°C	4 hours
Ginger root	Cut in 3mm slices	60°C	6 hours
Mangoes	Peeled, cut in 3mm slices, pit removed	60°C	6-8 hours
Mushrooms	Cleaned with soft brush (do not wash)	60°C	6-8 hours
Pineapple	Peeled, cored, cut in 3mm-1.25cm slices	60°C	6-8 hours
Strawberries	Cut in half or in 1.25cm slices	60°C	6-8 hours
Tomatoes	Cut in 3mm slices or grated; steam if planning to rehydrate	60°C	6-8 hours
MEAT, POULTRY, FISH			
Beef jerky	Cut in 6mm slices, marinated overnight	70°C	5-7 hours
Chicken jerky	Cut in 6mm slices, marinated overnight	70°C	5-7 hours
Salmon jerky	Cut in 6mm slices, marinated overnight	70°C	3-5 hours
Turkey jerky	Cut in 6mm slices, marinated overnight	70°C	5-7 hours

NOTE There is no temperature adjustment available or necessary when using the Max Crisp function.

Using DualZone Technology: SYNC

RECIPE	AMOUNT	MIX THESE INGREDIENTS	FUNCTION	TEMP/TIME
Fish Cakes	2 fish cakes	Brush with melted butter	Air Fry	200°C | 15 minutes
Balsamic Roasted Tomatoes	500g cherry tomatoes	60ml balsamic vinegar, 1 Tbsp vegetable oil	Roast	200°C | 15 minutes
Honey Sage Pork Chops	2-3 boneless pork chops (120g each)	1 Tbsp vegetable oil, 1 Tbsp honey	Roast	200°C | 17-20 minutes
Cajun Russet Potatoes	4 medium potatoes, diced	2 Tbsp vegetable oil, 2 Tbsp Cajun seasoning	Air Fry	200°C | 30 minutes
Green Beans with Almonds	500g green beans, ends trimmed	2 Tbsp vegetable oil, 60g sliced almonds	Air Fry	200°C | 8-10 minutes
Miso Glazed Salmon	3 salmon fillets (170g each)	2 Tbsp miso paste, 1 Tsp vegetable oil, rub onto salmon	Air Fry	200°C | 15 minutes
Honey Hazelnut Brussel Sprouts	500g Brussel sprouts, cut in half	2 Tbsp vegetable oil, 60ml honey, 60g chopped hazelnuts	Air Fry	200°C | 23 minutes
Buffalo Chicken Thighs	4 boneless skin-on chicken thighs (110-140g each)	240ml buffalo sauce, toss with chicken	Air Fry	200°C | 27 minute
Plant Based "Meat" Burger	500g plant-based ground "meat" (4 125g burgers)	1 Tbsp minced garlic, 1 Tbsp minced onion	Air Fry	190°C | 20 minute
Mediterranean Cauliflower	1 head cauliflower, cut in 1.5cm florets	120ml tahini, 2 Tbsp vegetable oil	Air Fry	200°C | 35 minutes
French Fries	500g French fries	Season as desired	Air Fry	200°C | 20 minutes
Corn on the cob	4 Cobettes	Brush with melted butter	Roast	180°C | 15 minutes

APPENDIX 2: RECIPES INDEX

Printed in Great Britain
by Amazon

25208343R00046